MAKING HAY

Books by Verlyn Klinkenborg

British Literary Manuscripts Series I and II
Making Hay
The Last Fine Time

MAKING HAY

Verlyn Klinkenborg

Illustrated by Gordon Allen

Guilford, Connecticut

An imprint of Globe Pequot

Distributed by NATIONAL BOOK NETWORK

British Library Cataloguing in Publication Information available

Library of Congress Cataloging-in-Publication Data available

Names: Verlyn Klinkenborg , author.
Title: Making Hay / Verlyn Klinkenborg.
Description: x, 157 p. : ill. ; 22 cm. ; Bibliography: pp. 155–157.
Identifiers: LCCN 86018550 (print) | ISBN 978-1-4930-3698-1 (paperback : alk. paper)
Subjects: Klinkenborg, Verlyn. Farm life—Middle West. Ranch life—Montana—Big Hole River Valley. Hay—Middle West. Hay—Montana—Big Hole River Valley.
Classification: S521.5.M53 K57 1986 (print) | DDC 630/.977
LC record available at https://lccn.loc.gov/86018550

Printed in the United States of America

To the memory of my mother,
HELEN CARLEY KLINKENBORG

PREFACE
to the 1997 Edition

I WROTE *Making Hay* in 1985 and early 1986 in a
sixth-floor apartment on Briggs Avenue in the Bronx.
Around the corner there was a Dominican grocery
and a Korean newsstand. The Grand Concourse ter-
minated nearby, and not far away the D and 4 trains
ran down to Manhattan. Eastward, at the foot of an
asphalt hill, lay the Botanical Garden stop on the
Metro North Railroad. From my office window, I
could look out over the rooftops of nearby houses and
see the traffic on Bedford Park Boulevard. The inti-
mate clatter of this part of the city—not such a very
busy place after all—rose to my window and filled the
small white room where I worked. My tiny corner of
the borough was not a neighborhood so much as a
parish with a saint's name, a place where all the significant landmarks were Catholic: the church on the
Concourse, the convent on the Boulevard, the university across the Avenue, even the precinct house on the
Parkway.

When I think of *Making Hay,* I think mainly of two things. I think of sitting in that small white room, learning to write, learning to attend to the specific gravity of words, to the wave-like energy that pulses through sentences, its rhythms shoaling and deepening, always in flux. And I think of driving along a gravel road in northwestern Iowa, learning to breathe again. The road marked a north/south crest in the landscape, like the edge of a moraine. Out the passenger window, to the east, Iowa held itself steady, level, a succession of townships receding in strict perspective toward the counties where I had grown up. But out the driver's-side window, the earth crumpled and fell away into a shallow river valley and climbed again. I was driving across what passes for upland in northwestern Iowa—not the Grant Wood hills, the erotic mounds and protuberances of eastern Iowa, but a rising shelf of soils upon which farmers wait, exposed, for the weather blowing in from the arid spaces to the west where cornfields turn to prairie and prairie turns to badlands and rimrock. A thunderstorm had just crowded past, and the air had been scoured clean. Water stood in the road, but the sun was already burning in a blue sky. The time was early June. The scent was of alfalfa.

For a dozen years or more, beginning in college, I had been a burrowing animal, living in libraries, occupying a small, book-lined den somewhere in the recesses of my skull. But on that trip to Iowa—returning to a childhood landscape after twenty years away— I could feel a transformation taking place. Picture a woodchuck coming out of its hole in the ground one morning and turning into a red-tailed hawk, or imagine a prairie dog suddenly metamorphosed into an antelope. That will give you some idea of the elation I felt at being back in the country. So will *Making Hay.* It's a book about farming, and it's a book, too, about a big change that blew over me when I was thirty-three. If *Making Hay* isn't quite as savvy, politically and agriculturally, as other things I've written since—things I've been able to write because of *Making Hay*—that is largely because I was too busy being overjoyed when I wrote it.

Some writers keep their works under revision all their lives, emending, reworking, and updating them every chance they get. But there's an old conceit among poets—to write a poem in which the author bids his book farewell. The spirit of that *bon voyage*—that *envoi*—seems right to me. It acknowledges not the perfection of the book—there is no such thing on earth—but its separateness. For every time I've wished I could revise *Making Hay,* there have been hundreds of times when I've wished *Making Hay* could revise me. And if it seems vain to talk about my own book this way, I can only say that *Making Hay* went its way in 1986, and whatever it has done since then has been done completely behind my back.

Making Hay is dedicated to the memory of my mother, who died on September 7, 1971, when she was forty-three. I would like to burnish that dedication and add to it. Elmore Jack Klinkenborg died in George, Iowa, on April 14, 1996, at the age of seventy-four. He was my uncle, and I am proud of it. This book is dedicated to his memory as well.

PREFACE

Making Hay IS A book about the work that farmers in the Midwest and ranchers in a Montana valley called the Big Hole do during the haying season. Because its subject is work, *Making Hay* is also about animals, machines, and the land.

I was raised in a small town in Iowa. My dad was a farmboy, and my mom was a farmgirl, though they grew up to be a teacher and a nurse. Most of my relatives on both sides of my family are or were farmers. Like farmers everywhere, and like the Big Hole's ranchers, they have suffered as the agricultural debt crisis has worsened. *Making Hay* is not about that crisis, not about banks, politics, economics, or erosion. It is about what keeps men and women farming despite the hard times: work, animals, machines, and the land. My aunts, uncles, and cousins are among the numerous cautious farmers who, though hurt by low prices, have not, so far, been threatened with loss of their farms or way of life. The same is true of the ranchers I met in Montana. The vast majority of farmers and ranchers belong to this group.

Making Hay is inevitably inflected by childhood memories and tempered by rediscoveries. After twenty years away from the Midwest, I found everything the same and everything different. The fields looked familiar, but the machines and the farms had changed. My aunts, uncles, and cousins had aged, as had I, but the relationship between experience and inexperience remained just as it was when I was a boy.

Why *Making Hay*? Why not *Making Corn*, or *Making Soybeans*, or *Making Oats*? Haying is what I always loved about the farm; alfalfa, far more than corn, summed up agriculture for me. It was raised and baled on the farm, fed on the farm, and spread as manure on the farm. No one ever trucked it away. It had the right smell. And rural life never looks better than when haying weather hits Minnesota, Iowa, or Montana.

ACKNOWLEDGMENTS

THIS BOOK COULD never have been written without the friendship and assistance of many people, especially those who let me poke around in their lives. Thanks, in the Midwest, go to Janelle and Louie Loger, Elmore Jack and Hilda Klinkenborg, Everon and Esther Klinkenborg, Dale Klinkenborg, Kerwin Klinkenborg, Myron and Mary Klinkenborg, Randy Klinkenborg, Davis Klinkenborg, Ken and Frieda Klinkenborg, and Jim Klinkenborg.

Thanks, in Montana, go to Russ, Pat, and Shirley Peterson, Fred, Vera, Jerry, and Dale Rutledge, Frank Stanchfield, Dave and Chris Decker of The Complete Fly Fisher in Wise River, who took fine care of Reggie and me during haying season, Craig and Peggy Fellin of Big Hole Outfitters in Wise River, Rich and Shirley Shepherd, Julie Davies, Ruthmary Tonn of the Voss Inn in Bozeman, and Craig and Jackie Mathews of Blue Ribbon Flies in West Yellowstone.

I have received technical assistance from a number of persons, all of them generous with their time and ideas: Earl Hudson, John Richardson, Ed Blakeslee, Ken Smith, Ray Ditterline and D. K. Barnes. Needless to say, none of them is responsible for my errors of fact or implication.

I also want to thank readers and commentators: Eric Sigg, Steve and Ellen Polansky, Elizabeth Doxsee, Bobbie Bristol, and John and Jill Klinkenborg.

Finally, I want to express my gratitude to several people who have supported the idea of this book from the start: my publisher, Nick Lyons, my dad, Ronald Klinkenborg, and, most important of all, my wife, Reggie Wenzek, whose good humor and affection have been unfailing.

MAKING HAY

1

ELMORE JACK KNOWS A man who once had a quadruple-bypass. After the operation, his doctor suggested he walk three or four miles a day. In the spring, summer, and fall he hikes in his neighborhood and through the adjoining countryside, but during the heavy Iowa winter Elmore Jack's friend drives to the mall, where he walks back and forth between department stores, past the poster shops and cookie stands and smoked cheese boutiques. A quadruple-bypass has led him into temptation.

He should come instead to the VFW lounge in Luverne, Minnesota, twelve miles east of South Dakota, ten miles north of Iowa. Twice around the dance floor and Elmore Jack's friend would have pegged his three miles. Twice around the dance floor in the stiff-waisted polka they are doing here this June Saturday night and he might never need to walk again.

When Elmore Jack waltzes with Hilda, striding over the springy floor, he turns his knees loose and lets them manage the three-four. He and Hilda appear to have different theories of dancing, though they move well together, husband and wife. If they were swinging axes, their motions would be just as dissimilar. Elmore Jack would let the blade fall lazily from its apogee into the heartwood, flicking it at the end; Hilda would command the axe-head downward with the force of her powerful spirit. It is hard to say who would split more elm. It is also hard to say who looks more natural doing the Chicken Dance.

The music still, Elmore Jack leans over. His bolo tie swings forward, and he gestures with a closed hand. He is explaining his presence here on most Saturday nights of the year. He talks slowly in a friendly, fuzzy voice, while behind him a human Zamboni walks over the empty floor, scattering dance wax.

"I'm a lifetime member of this VFW post, which is one of the biggest in the Midwest. Started driving up here in forty-six when I got out of the service, and we've been coming now for thirty-nine years. Always came to Luverne, even though we live in Iowa. Minnesota posts are just more fun than Iowa ones. Nellie has a standing reservation for our table, but if we're not here by eight-fifteen, she gives it to someone else."

Nellie, a slender, familiar woman, has stopped by twice tonight with rounds of bourbon, whiskey, beer, and popcorn for the crowd where Elmore Jack sits. This is not his regular table; he has come over to join his sister, Janelle, Janelle's husband Louie, and their guests—two of his nephews (I am one), their wives, and his youngest brother (my father), who lives in California now.

Elmore Jack says wait a minute and digs in his wallet.

"They give life members a metal card."

He tosses it onto the table and it lands with a clank. It says E. J. Klinkenborg in bas relief and looks like the plaque on a Civil War Memorial. The VFW apparently wants all its life members to have at least one bulletproof means of identification.

In the parking lot everyone swore this was a slow night, but the dance floor is filled with bodies. Sometimes the dancers—sixty-five, seventy couples—move in wide, pelagic motion, and sometimes, to the faster tunes, it looks like a bee dance on a hive's lip. The Larry Olsen Band has only three pieces: a young blonde wearing a vermilion pant-suit and playing a synthesizer bass, a middle-aged drummer aided on percussion by the swishing from the dancers' feet, and a seated accordionist who sings in a flat Minnesota accent. He carries a tune well, but he could double as a Sioux Falls livestock auctioneer during the week. The Larry Olsen Band has its fans: two couples wearing vests, two red, two white, which say The Larry Olsen Fan Club in bowling script. Why the different colors, no one is sure. Seniority, I guess.

Elmore Jack takes Reggie, my wife, out on the floor for the Circle Two-Step Mixer. Partner is passed to

3

partner like a loose electron. Half the men out there wear cowboy boots under pressed bell-bottoms, maybe ten of the women wear square-dance dresses and fancy dancing panties. Nearly all the men have pale foreheads and deeply tanned jaws—a farmer's tattoo. With their hats off, you can no longer tell at a glance what herbicide they use. A few have heavy girths hiding underslung beltlines. As the couples whirl round, you can see every now and then resting on a woman's waist a dark hand with a missing digit—victim of auger, baler, elevator, silage wagon, manure spreader, combine, corn sheller, feed grinder, or chainsaw.

These are veteran couples every one. They look as though the sharp years of conflict were no match for steady farming. They move abundantly through the darkness. In the distant right corner a semi-circular bar fills with non-Circle-Two-Steppers. We passed a second bar as we walked in, and Nellie draws her drinks from another. An unseen bar is hidden in the back below the curvature of the earth. Only the tops of the patrons' heads are visible, like fence posts across a late-June corn-field.

The scene at the VFW renews the sensation you get as you drive across midwestern farmland. However the terrain tips and rolls, however the fences and runoffs mark a field, whether the soil carries soybeans, sorghum, corn, oats, or alfalfa, the black earth has only one pur-pose: getting the crops up. Some of these farmers left their tractors in the fields, some parked them in brand-new Butler buildings or converted granaries, but they all came dancing amidst identical tasks. All the tractors they used today, wherever they sit, will wear corn-

sprayers Monday. The details of their farms differ, but not their essentials. The community of farmers as a whole is not here, but their intent is well represented.

Two nights ago a heavy storm blew through. A tornado touched earth just south of Rock Rapids. Near George, not far from Elmore Jack and Hilda's farm, three inches of rain fell; in another part of Lyon County, only an eighth of an inch. We were on the road in the dark that night driving home after the storm from a wedding anniversary and reunion in Lester. Ordinarily, the distant lights of farmyards and the ridged gravel roads keep a driver's attention, but that night the moon was out, and it shone off the muddy water that had gathered in the fields and was hissing through culverts. It takes a storm like that to disturb the synchrony of farming. Some men would now replant beans when they could. Some would think about sowing sorghum in the smooth patches where the corn had washed out. Those farmers who had not put drains in their low fields would once again consider doing so, adding up the cost of backhoe and tile in their minds. Tonight still the fields are too wet for anything but dancing at the VFW.

The tempo seems to increase, Reggie disappears in a wood of friendly faces blowing this way and that, Larry Olsen spits out wafer-thin syllables about love and comic romance, men greet friends and strangers happily as they bump in and out of the bathroom, and the dear dead of this VFW post look down from the walls as Nellie makes another round, bringing only soft drinks to our table—two stiff ones is enough any Saturday night.

Suddenly, in a great roar of laughter, the Circle

Two-Step Mixer ends and Elmore Jack and Reggie return to the table from separate corners of the floor. Reggie's final partner was the dreaded toe-dancer, a foppish perfectionist who has a pronounced heel-lift when he walks and whom Hilda reviles, smiling severely, the moment he is mentioned.

"Oh ya, he and his wife, they drive fifty, sixty miles here every Saturday night, and when they're done dancing, they sit back down at their table and go over her mistakes. He draws the dances on a napkin, honey."

Reggie says that when the Circle Two-Step ended, her partner threw himself down on one knee, thanked her ma'am, and begged to escort her back to her table. Elmore Jack and everyone else laughs. The toe-dancer and his wife must practice in a picture window off Main Street somewhere. Farmers dance, they don't demonstrate.

As we get up to leave, Larry Olsen is singing a polka favorite.

> In heaven there is no beer
> That's why we drink it here
> And when we're gone from here
> Our friends will be drinking all the beer.

The young woman playing bass turns around and grins at the drummer. A twelve-year-old girl with long ankles and a short waist is dancing with her mother and singing along.

It is traditional to stop at Country Kitchen, just south of the VFW, after a night's dancing. We gather around a formica table for decaf coffee, pecan pie, and sweet rolls the size of chuck roasts, which arrive on hot steak platters. There is desultory conversation. My uncle Elmore Jack asks my uncle Louie about the new sickle blade for his windrower.

"Damn thing didn't fit," Louie says.

"What'd you do?"

"Fixed it. Put a new head on."

To all pie-eaters, Hilda says, "How's the pecan pie, honey?"

The weather has been good since the storm. The moon is nearly three-quarters full. Where it showed us standing water two nights ago, it now illuminates glossy mudflats along corner fencelines. The Rock River is up by nearly a foot, and its sharply cut banks will yield more sod to the current overnight. From Luverne, it is five miles south to Janelle and Louie's farm along a shallow ridge above the Rock River. Kicking gravel into its fender skirts, the car clatters past dark clumps of farmsteads. The air fills with pig scent, then cow scent, and then the blended sweetness of vegetation. We pass the place that has nine kids, geese, turkeys, horses, pigs, and milk cows and we are almost home. We come to the solitary crib. Down in the valley, the Rock River catches the night's gleam. Even in the dark, we know the fields around here because Louie, who will make pink squirrels when we get to the house, has taught them to us. The corn is half a foot high, the soybeans are newly leaved, the oats are in boot, and Alfalfa, Queen of Legumes, is in early bloom. It is time to make hay.

2

MORE THAN MOST farmers, Louie appreciates the dramatic effect of understatement. When he said he fixed the sickle on his windrower, his words did not do justice to the fact. In 1969, he and Janelle bought a three-hundred-and-twenty-acre farm in Clinton Township of Rock County, Minnesota. The house was in good shape, but it had only a half-cellar—a shallow, dirt-floored cavity. So they put in a new basement. When I asked Louie how they had inserted a poolroom, bar, utility room, shower, and pantry under a two-story, four-bedroom farmhouse, he said, "Jacked it up."

Louie's terseness may have come down through his own family, the Logers, but marrying into a loquacious clan has tightened it even further. At the regular family gatherings that took place Sunday afternoons at the Klinkenborg *pater familias* place in George, Iowa, during the fifties and early sixties, the men played pinochle in a small chamber set off from the living room by oak half-columns, away from the women who thundered through the kitchen and dining room, bearing dried beef, potato rolls, jello salads, and divinity. It seems to be a Klinkenborg trait, even over pinochle, to talk until you run out of words and then to look around somewhat perplexedly for verbal supplies. I remember Louie, black-haired, small next to his gangly brothers-in-law and nephews, smoking, waiting, and then when an absence of words had afflicted the lot of them, saying something like "Jacked it up" and bringing the house down. He would look at one of the kids who watched the play of cards and smile, as if to say, "Ain't these grownups something?"

I mention this because when I began to help Louie around the farm, I accidentally converted the work, by my mere presence, into a public act. Their two sons grown and departed, Louie and Janelle farm alone. They spend the greater part of the day at separate tasks, and though most of the work occurs outdoors it is essentially private, silent except for the inarticulate roar of machinery. Janelle talks to Sam the dog—himself an emblem of taciturnity because all their dogs have been called Sam. Louie yells at the cows, perhaps for their comfort as much as his. What they do not have, day in, day out, is an extra Klinkenborg running around asking questions.

Friday was wet, with none of the spectacular cloud

effects of Thursday, the day of the big storm. No rainbows, no tornadoes, no domes in an evening sky, just a settled breezy rain. Even if we got the windrower repaired it would be a day or two before we could cut alfalfa. After breakfast and chores, Louie walked down to the old hipped building where he keeps his less frequently employed machinery. The shed smelled of a penetrating mix of diesel fuel, machine oil, gasoline, straw, and the pulverized dust of dirt that has gone to mud once too often. In the dark end of the building near his corn planter, Louie climbed onto the windrower and started it up with a cough. He edged it through the door, and the four-cylinder din dropped off in damp open air.

Because Janelle and Louie's farm lies on river bottomland, it has more grade to it than most midwestern farms. The drive into their place used to be a through road that sloped down to the Rock River and crossed an iron bridge long since washed away. (The county finally got around to designating Janelle and Louie's drive a dead-end road two years ago. Until then they regularly saw unannounced, bewildered visitors.) The drop from the blacktop county highway through the farmyard and down to the river makes a pretty fair hill, enough that the highest part of their alfalfa field is taller by a silo's height than the corn fields that reach right down to the river's crumbling edge.

Louie throttled the windrower up the farmyard's terraced grade. At the low end of the yard lies the hipped machine shed and an old cookhouse, a hot-weather kitchen annex that stood near the well when the farm was first built. Above those buildings rise a granary, silo, and calf barn, once a dairy barn, far and away the oldest structure on the place. Then come disused chicken and hog houses, where the family farrowed sows, and finally the modern machine shop, on the same level as the house. The highest structures are not properly buildings: a pair of Butler corn dryers perch on the edge of the alfalfa field above the house. Louie wheeled the windrower around and backed it into the shop, next to his Vermeer round baler, his International Harvester feedgrinder, and an IH 656 tractor with front-loader. He eased off the throttle, raised the cutter-bar and reel together, then lifted the reel higher still. Louie killed the ignition, looked at me with a grin, and after the engine's echo had stopped bouncing off the corrugated steel walls said, "Well?"

A townboy on the farm tends to admire agricultural machinery not for what it will do to crops but for what it will do to the poor soul who falls down in front of it. I was so primed with outlandish warnings when I stayed on the farm as a kid that they crept back into my head unbidden at the sight of Louie's windrower. Like a combine (I could hear my cousins say), it would cut you off at the ankles, grab you in its steel fingers, toss you onto a canvas conveyer belt which would then, unlike a combine, drop you on the ground, only to pick you up and crush you with a pair of heavy rollers and drop you on the ground again. Then your bones could bleach in peace in a nice, orderly pile until the baling crew came along some sunny day and tossed you into the fenceline or tacked you up inside the barn door next to the raccoon skull. In my childhood it took three machines —mower, crimper, siderake—to achieve the same results.

A windrower, or swather, as some farmers call it, represents the historical tendency of agricultural engineers to combine the functions of several tools in a single machine. The most famous and aptly named example of that inclination, the combine itself, reaps and threshes and eliminates such chores as the binding of bundles and the building of shocks and the sacking of grain. The right way to appraise a modern self-propelled combine, which is about as easy to park in a crowded machine shed as a Spanish galleon, is to think of it not as replacing a certain number of hand tasks—long outmoded by the time the combine appeared in the 1940s—but as summing up all the machines that preceded it. In its bulk it incorporates the Hussey and McCormick reapers of the early nineteenth century, the self-binders, the horse-power flail, the forty-horse-team combined harvesters of the turn-of-the-century Palouse, and the horse-powered, steam-powered, or gas-powered stationary threshing machine, which looks like nothing so much as a beaten tin belt-driven brontosaurus. Louie does not own a combine. Bruce, his neighbor, does. So Louie windrows for Bruce, and Bruce does Louie's combining. When I asked Louie what the exchange rate for windrowing and combining was, he said, "We work it out."

Like so much agricultural machinery, a windrower looks simple because its design blatantly expresses its function. It does what it looks like it should. It cuts a wide swath of alfalfa, crushes it, and leaves behind a crop line, or windrow, narrow enough for a forage chopper or baler. Agricultural design tends to stability. Farm engineering has not altered fundamental tools; it has applied power to them. Horsepower has increased, speeds have bounded, functions have diversified, but farming remains largely a matter of dragging, poking, jabbing, tearing, slicing, chopping, separating, and transporting. The basic tools for those tasks have not changed since the early nineteenth century. The transition from scythe to horse-drawn reaper in the 1840s and 50s was a more radical shift in tool design than the change from reaper to windrower.

To get a clear picture of a windrower, imagine a small tractor that mainly goes backward. The driver's seat faces what is usually the rear, and front is back, right is left. Broaden the axle length of those large driving wheels; make the tires smaller, too. Reverse the steering mechanism so the driving wheels also turn the machine and make the tail wheels merely free-spinning casters. Spread or offset those tail wheels so they don't crumple or scatter the windrowed crop. Increase the weight of the tail (formerly the nose) by adding concrete ballast to counterbalance the machinery that must be added to the front, ahead of the driver's seat and driving wheels. What you have is no longer a tractor because it pushes instead of pulling.

Mount a header in front of the driving wheels. Early headers, patented in the 1840s, were cumbersome harvesters pushed rather than drawn by horses, which carried the cut grain up a conveyer into a wagon. They were called headers because they cut off only the tops, or heads, of the grain. (Most reapers, in contrast, were pulled by horses, cut the grain off near the soil, and deposited it loose or in bundles on the ground.) The header on a modern windrower performs four separate tasks. Each is simple in itself, but together they require a complex system of belts, pulleys, hydraulics, and gears, mostly shielded under metal guards painted a trademark color: green for John Deere, red or white for International Harvester, red or yellow for New Holland.

First the sickle blade chops off the alfalfa near the ground. (The windrower's four to nine-mile-per-hour forward speed helps greatly here.) To force the alfalfa to fall neatly, a long reel with protruding steel fingers urges the plants onto the knives. The reel is as long as the blade, anywhere from ten to sixteen feet, with a diameter of about five feet, and moves like a vastly elongated ferris wheel, reaching down into the standing crop, pushing it past the knives, and coercing it onto the conveyer that transports and organizes the crop.

If a windrower uses an auger to carry cut alfalfa it has an auger header; if it uses wood-slatted canvas belts, it is called a draper header. (Early reapers and most modern grain windrowers use draper headers.) The conveyer reduces the swath from the blade width (ten to sixteen feet) to the width a baler can pick up—usually about three feet. It shuttles alfalfa from both sides of the header and feeds it through a narrow gap in the center to the header's fourth major tool: the crimper or crusher. This is nothing more than an old-fashioned washing-machine wringer of huge proportions. Its two rollers, rubber or steel, intermesh in patented ways. A New Holland windrower, for instance, has rollers which, if inked and fed with paper, would print an interlocking zig-zag design. These rollers wreak a terrible fate on alfalfa, crimping or crushing the stems in order to make them more palatable to cattle and to force the crop to dry faster. After it has been "conditioned" by the crimper, alfalfa desiccates with despair.

14

This basic machine, first bought in significant numbers in the 1960s, ag engineers have subtly refined to
keep pace with improvements made to other field implements. Most windrower companies have added closed
cabs with air conditioning to cut down on dust and
noise. Some have switched from mechanical gear boxes
to hydrostatic drives, which propel the machine by means
of a closed-circuit high-pressure hydraulics system that
assures smooth power flow at somewhat decreased fuel
efficiency. New Holland patented a twin sickle drive;
instead of one set of gears impelling a single long blade,
two sets of gears, mounted on either side of the header,
impel two half-width blades, increasing knife speeds.
This, in the language of ag engineers, is an "aggressive"
design.

By these standards, Louie's windrower, a 1979 International Harvester 230, is an old-fashioned machine.

Louie sits exposed to breezes, bugs, and sun in an open cockpit. (He owns only one closed-cab implement: an International Harvester 1066 tractor, which was in a neighbor's shop having its air-conditioning repaired. A closed cab without air-conditioning is a sweatbox.) His alfalfa falls to a single long sickle blade. The IH 230 has a variable-speed belt drive instead of hydrostatic power. It also has a draper header, whose canvases wear out. Before we started work on the sickle blade, we spent two hours one morning installing a pair of canvases, which a man in town had patched for seventy-six dollars.

Most outmoded of all, it has a Caterpillar-like or differential steering system. Two tall levers rise before the driver's seat. One controls the motion of the left wheel, the other the motion of the right wheel. By urging the left forward and the right rearward, or vice versa, Louie can make the windrower gyrate completely in its own length. It steers with the violent, accusatory motions of a tank. As one engineer put it, operating a windrower with differential steering is "like rowing a boat all day long," because the driver is perpetually compensating for one move after another. Advanced windrowers have a steering wheel and power-assist steering, no less comfortable to drive than a Cadillac Coupe de Ville with a fifteen-foot grass saw welded to its grille, and not a cent less expensive, either.

As rain gusted off the shop roof, Louie and I stared into the exposed maw of his machine. When the windrower is running, a fifteen-foot row of serrated, trapezoidal knives bolted in threes to a long steel bar slides between finger guards like the blade of an electric knife. But the sickle blade has been worn down by use. When Louie cut Bruce's alfalfa in late May, two weeks ago, the windrower lugged its way through the field, burning too much fuel and cutting laboriously. Louie had planned to replace the sickle blade before that cut, but the new blade had not arrived, even though Janelle had ordered it nearly six months earlier. Out of patience at last, he drove to Windom, Minnesota—sixty miles away—during the storm on Thursday and plucked his new sickle blade off a loading dock, where it would have sat until a full truck was made up for Luverne. It cost six hundred and fifty dollars. A fifteen-foot serrated sickle blade is almost impossible to sharpen and only slightly more difficult to replace.

The first step was to remove the old blades by sliding out the sickle bar to which they were bolted. Louie handed me an impact wrench—a compressed-air socket driver—pointed to a long row of bolts holding on the guards of the blade and said, "Loosen them nuts." I did so and began to appreciate the routine strength of farmers. When I tried to torque the nuts from the steel, the nuts tried to torque the wrench from my hand. The old blade, chipped and dulled and stained with mud and alfalfa, slid out easily. Then I tightened them nuts on the new guards. We opened the box the RazorCat was shipped in. The blade looked like a fifteen-foot platinum diamondback rattler sliced in half longitudinally. It wobbled as we picked it up and gave off evil airs. There were repeated warnings: watch your hands, watch your head.

After forty-five minutes of pushing, prying, eye-balling, but remarkably little swearing, we got the new blade through the guards and in place. It did not fit. A foot and a half of knife edges protruded. That could be cut off with a torch. Worse, the reinforced head of the blade, which bolts to a wristlike pivot that rocks the blade back and forth through the guards, missed matching its bolt holes by nearly two inches. This would be harder to fix.

Louie smiled impatiently. He uttered his worst imprecation, a calm "shit." I could think only of sending the blade back to the manufacturer for a refund. Janelle, who had come out of the house, laughed.

Coffee is hot in the kitchen, and the twinkie cake is cool. There will be a short break followed by down time.

3

OCTOBER, IT IS snowing at Forty Bar Ranch in the Big Hole of Montana. Isolated squalls coast up and down the basin from the Hairpin Ranch at the southern extreme all the way north to the Pintler Wilderness. They swamp the draws on the slopes and race along the water seams between cottonwood, aspen, and willow on the valley floor. From far away the clouds seem to drag on the earth, their tops cantilevered by the wind.

Up in the timber, it has already drifted heavily. When a badger kills a ground squirrel he runs on the Twin Lakes road for easy traveling, his load in his mouth. The cattle have begun to move to lower pastures out of the heavy willows where the moose browse. On the valley bottom, Doug and M.D. are building a new bridge to replace the old plank one over the main stem of the Big Hole River. Farther downstream, well below Wisdom, the Big Hole is frozen clear across in spots.

This new bridge is no plank affair. It takes a crane, a D8 Cat, a dump truck, and a small crew from Dillon to construct because it is made from railroad flatcars, two of them, with their trucks removed. They sit on pilings over a one-lane river. The road crossing the flow here starts as a turnoff from Highway 278. It runs down among the buildings of Forty Bar Ranch, frays into a dozen tracks, skirts a triple line of massive haystacks, and peters out in a cowpath a couple haymeadows up. Follow that path carefully enough and it would take you over the Bitterroot Mountains and into Idaho.

The crane roars and shoots a black tube of smoke cloudward. Midspan, Doug does the welder's nod to flip his faceshield down, and the acetylene torch flares. The Cat, which they have had trouble starting, sputters into action along the streambed. There is no sense of urgency in this work; it is the kind of task that ranchers take on between big jobs—say, calving and haying. The gelid fringes on the fast-running river and the clattering of the aspens around Unc and Mom's place, over by the cookhouse, look and sound wintry, but there are one or two thaws still left in this autumn before the hard freeze comes. Despite the snow, Russ has time to think about building a sloping bin for the grain shed so he won't have to shovel pellets off the concrete floor into the auger. His daughter Shirley has time to knock off log-splitting and show me around. Her cousin Gary keeps the chainsaw running. There isn't *that* much time, not for young male cousins at least.

Shirley is a dental hygienist in Pocatello, home for a long weekend. She is engaged to marry a man named Joe, who does industrial work for the state of Idaho. She and Joe talk about living in Alaska, for which she has been well prepared by growing up at the Ajax and Forty Bar Ranch. Shirley is a slim woman in her early twenties with light brown hair, pretty from the outdoors and the weather, her skin a little tougher than her age. Like her father, she warms to strangers slowly but thoroughly. It is worth the wait to see her smile. Her mother, Pat, is downright adoptive in nature, her brothers, Doug and M.D., just plain shy. (Russ and Pat's younger daughter Jeanine is in nursing school at Missoula.)

The bridge crew waves (Doug waggles the torch) when we bump over the old plank structure in Shirley's red Subaru. The river, naturally, marks the low center of the valley, which is much broader than it looks from the highway cutting south along the east side. On the bridge—surrounded by the river's switchbacks, willow banks, and a web of cattle yards, haymeadows, and irrigation canals—one's visibility on the horizontal halts at about sixty yards. That is why the Petersons put their new house up by the highway: less trouble getting out in the snow, and a view from the dining room table that seems to take in most of Beaverhead County. Over coffee, you can see Homer Young, Copperhead, and Ajax Peaks. You can practically sight the tailings of the old Ajax Mine.

We don't spot Russ until we meet him at a gate. He is driving a closed-cab Case tractor and pulling a wagon with sideracks of peeled logs, full of green summer hay. Russ is a good-sized man, getting more so around the middle. He attributes his roundness to quitting smoking and Darlene the cook. He has the Peterson nose, a little on the large side, same as Unc (his uncle Melvin), and under it a black, gray-flecked moustache. He wears a flannel cowboy shirt, red suspenders, jeans, work boots, and an insulated Dillon Fertilizer cap. For a native Montanan he chews tobacco with remarkable restraint. Russ resembles his grandfather, Sam. Unc showed me a photograph taken just after the turn of the century. There sits Sam, upright and stout, on horseback in the dirt streets of Dillon. He is wearing a coat and tie.

Behind the gate Russ came through is the second reason Sam Peterson walked from Anaconda, where he worked on the smelter, into the Big Hole to homestead: hay, tons and tons of it, mounded in huge stacks. We can hear Sam's first reason mooing all around us, though the herds are hidden by fence and willow. The Forty Bar, like every other ranch in the Big Hole, is a cattle operation. Like every other ranch in the Big Hole, the Forty Bar has most of its land in haymeadow (whatever is not sagebrush, pine forest, and willow swamp) and it has seen better days.

In the Big Hole they reduce the hay/cattle relationship to its essentials: one crop—hay—and one cash source, cattle. They don't fool around with soybeans, sorghum, oats, corn, or other such nonsense, though they once made cheese here. Hay and cattle and some horses for moving the cattle down off the mountains. They do not even fuss with alfalfa here; they grow wild hay. Or rather, *they* do not grow wild hay, the valley does, as it has since long before Lewis and Clark arrived and found Indians summering their horses here in the rich native pastures along the river.

Most of the haymeadows in the Big Hole have neither been tilled nor sown in decades, but some get a touch of fertilizer (from trucks, not tractors) in October. Year after year, the soil carries timothy, redtop, bluejoint, nutgrass, a couple of fescues, creeping and meadow foxtails, clovers, and bromegrass, as well as some miscellaneous rushes and sedges (called sloughgrass locally) in the damp spots. When a midwestern steer has finished the alfalfa entrée, it needs a grain or silage course because alfalfa is high in protein and low in energy. When a Big Hole steer has finished the wild hay menu, it is done eating period until it disembarks from the semi in Minnesota or Nebraska.

During Russ's fifty-some years in the Big Hole, the hay crop has never failed, and even Unc (the twin of Russ's father, Elvin), born in 1906, cannot recall a lapse. There have been times when one rancher had to borrow a stack from another rancher, but most years they go into winter with leftovers from last winter to boot. Nineteen eighty-five has been the driest summer in Russ's memory. So the grasses can dry and the ground can firm, ranchers normally turn off the water in the irrigation ditches ten days before they mow the meadows in early August. This year the water simply disappeared two weeks before they usually divert it. Still, and to Russ's surprise, his mixed-breed herds, grazed on pasture through the hot months, are as sleek and fat as they have ever been. When we drive down the cowpaths, they bound out of our way only after we have chased them for a dozen yards. From the rear, they look like burros slung with cattle-colored panniers of grass.

Wild hay is grown in only a few high-altitude locations in the West—places like the Big Hole, at 6,200 feet above sea level, and Henry's Lake Flat, and several mountain valleys in Montana, Colorado, and Wyoming. A number of things conspire against alfalfa in these places: the wet soil, which alfalfa will not tolerate, the short growing season, the harsh winters, and the fact that winter-hardy alfalfas—those that can stand severe winters (and, as a side effect, yield less than nonhardy strains)—do not produce the bulk of hay required for the numbers of cattle these ranchers run. And then there is the question of nutritional completeness. No Big Hole rancher is about to start purchasing the quantities of silage or grain needed to supplement alfalfa. Ninety-day corn won't grow at 6,200 feet.

Partly because of these constraints, the Big Hole is a haven of traditionalism. That places it squarely at odds with the agricultural advice apparatus in this country. I talked to one member of that apparatus who began by mentioning the Big Hole's traditionalism. "It's like stepping a hundred years back in time up there," he said. "Some of those stands of grass are forty years old." The tone of his voice made it clear he found no charm in antique ranching. "They've got piss-poor irrigation practices. They turn the water on and leave it on. It's a swamp up there, the only place in the country where they farm sloughgrass." And then there are the haymaking practices themselves. "They wait till the grass has headed [produced seed] before they mow. By then, the plant has lignified—it's trying to become a tree. They get higher bulk, but nutrition goes to hell in a handbasket. So they have to feed higher volume."

This makes sense in an office, and it probably even figures on a calculator, but it does not tally in the Big

24

Hole. The economics and technology of haying there weigh against change. Ranchers have at their feet a perennial source of nutrition that demands none of the ecological compromises of large-scale midwestern farming. Wild hay does require feeding higher volumes than alfalfa, but then the higher volumes are there for the taking. The only trick is that you have to put the hay up quickly and you have to put it up by the hundreds of tons. To do that you need special machines and you need people.

In October, the Forty Bar is almost ghostly with the hint of absent haying crews. The arrow weathervane on the log horsebarn's cupola seems to point in a direction the wind once sat and can sit no longer. The south side of the horsebarn is hung with harnesses from the days when a hundred and fifty horses grazed east of the Jackson road, nearly all of them used to pull Case or McCormick & Deering mowers or push buckrakes or draw haywagons or work the Mormon derricks or overshot stackers or beaverslides. A bear skull hangs beside the tack. Beds in the red bunkhouses are covered with newspaper and the stoves are clean of ashes, pegs free of jeans, porches of boots. Out along the fence marking the farthest perimeter of buildings, thorns grow between the floorboards of an old beaverslide hoist and poke through the perforated iron seat of an early Farmall—the kind that sold with iron-lugged wheels.

Because the past is so much present in the Big Hole, it is too easy to notice the things that have been lost with time. The things that have been saved are more important, and among those is native ingenuity. They store ingenuity in sheds and stack it along fencelines it is so abundant at the Forty Bar. To make hay in the Big Hole, you need, in the order they are used: 1. sickle-blade mowers, to cut the hay; 2. siderakes, or, as they call them here, wheelrakes or greenrakes, to windrow the hay; 3. buckrakes, to push the windrows into huge piles and load the beaverslide; 4. dump or crazyrakes, to clean the corners of the field and pick up scattered hay; 5. a hoist, to raise and lower the basket on the beaverslide; 6. a beaverslide, to build the stack (more about that later); and 7. a Cat, to move the beaverslide. You also need tractors to pull the mowers and wheel-rakes and crazyrakes. In winter you need hayforks to load haywagons with hay from haystacks to feed cattle. A tractor powers the hayfork and pulls the haywagon, except when diesel fuel gels in the fifty below. Then they use pitchforks and horses and haysleds, the old way.

Of all these implements, only the Cat and the trac-tors (and the oldest mowers) are not made in the Big Hole. The Petersons own one new Case, an older Ford, and half a dozen Farmall Cs and Ms and Hs—thirty-year-old machines that have not been seen in the Mid-west, where they stay strictly current on such things, in decades. (There was even, tucked away in one small shed with the cool autumn light on its warm red paint, a Farmall B on the Forty Bar—a tiny tractor with an offset steering column—the first machine I learned how to drive.) These Farmalls were not built in the Big Hole, but they have all been rebuilt there. When you do not have to tear up the earth, you do not need three-hundred-horse articulated four-wheel-drive tractors. An ancient C will pull a modern Big Hole wheelrake, provided you have the ingenuity to add hydraulics to the tractor. They do in Jackson.

Shirley took me through all the sheds, opening a different kind of latch at every one. Latches and gates are a subspecies of Forty Bar ingenuity. Each building Shirley and I entered had a different contraption holding the door shut. Nearly every gate we opened swung on a different kind of hinge, most fashioned from iron rings and wooden boxes. (The commonest gate latch was a horseshoe on a chain.) We walked past a homemade logsplitter where Russ and the boys shiver kindling for Russ's mom's woodstove, on which she still cooks. We cut around buckboards and green propane tanks and even, occasionally, the shank bone of a heifer and once a cow skull, still partly fleshed, that lacked a lower jaw. A dead mouse in a feed bucket bothered Shirley more than these.

One red shed held a new breed of double-sickle mower, built in Jackson. In an old log workshop we saw piles of sickle blades and a sharpening jig with an adjustable guide angle. During the mowing, sickle blades are pulled off the mowers at noon, loaded into the pickup Pat uses to carry dinners and sharp blades to the field, and brought back here, where one man sharpens all day long. (These are not serrated knives so they sharpen well.) In another shed we found four buckrakes, one of them only a season old, sleek Jackson-built machines, agricultural hot rods.

Behind the sheds rested half a dozen bright green wheelrakes (hence greenrakes), each carrying twelve huge steel wheels with forty yellow spring tines projecting outward like the sun's corona. Along one fence lay a row of thirteen-tined wooden rakes that resemble gates with teeth and bolt to the front of buckrakes. We saw three dismounted hayforks that looked like tyrannosaurus talons. Hayforks are huge steel arms with shoulder, elbow, and wrist joints that manipulate talons, which reach up and clutch a dinosaur's handful of hay from the stack and then pivot to drop it in a haywagon or feedbunk. Doug built the one mounted on the Case. Four hydraulics lines and an immense chain and sprocket maneuver it. The only thing that marks it as a home-made tool is the lack of a manufacturer's decal. As long as Doug is around, it has a lifetime warranty.

Shirley grinned as she opened one red machine shed. It sheltered a snowplane. Someone, no one remembered who, had built a closed fuselage-like shell on skis with an airplane engine and prop mounted at the rear. When winter sat deep on the Ajax, where Shirley grew up half a dozen miles from the road, they used the snowplane to reach the bus. But as Russ later told me, there were lots of ancillary snowplane sports, like impressing the womenfolk by chasing moose into the yard. They ceased to be impressed, he admitted, if you bagged one with a snowplane's prop, as he once did by accident.

The other buildings on the floor of the Forty Bar were part domestic, part utilitarian. A white clapboard cookhouse for Darlene with a Vulcan restaurant stove, a meat locker, and a walk-in freezer (a sign inside the door says "You Are Not Locked In"), a white clapboard bunkhouse for Doug, M.D., and, temporarily, Gary, a white clapboard house set off by a low wire fence and a border of aspen for Unc and Mom. An aquamarine corrugated-steel machine shop, a corrugated-steel calv-ing barn with a veterinary supplies room and a dozen stalls and operating theater lights where M.D. could do Caesareans on cattle if needed. A small log shed with

an iron box stove set at the back above the flume that runs through the feedlots. The stove is stoked in the winter so water keeps flowing to the cattle. (One of those basic problems: how do you water cattle when it's twenty below?) And set aside in apparent neglect, the house, a square-logged, lime-chinked, sod-roofed cabin, where Russ's father Elvin and his twin brother Melvin were born in February 1906. The cabin would fit in the living room of the main house. It looks as if they once called it a midwiving shed.

Shirley and I bump across the old plank bridge in her Subaru one last time. We are headed out to the haystacks, which have somehow migrated from the scattered haymeadows where they rose into a neat line just beyond the river. "Somehow" is one of those problems they answer in the Big Hole with hydraulics and steel. Shirley showed me a stackmover—one of three in the valley, the first built about 1967. Then she took me over to their brand-new beaverslide. Like the Peterson wheelrakes, the metal reinforcement on their beaverslide is bright green, the trademark color of Rich Shepherd, the local genius who builds these tools at his garage in Jackson. The beaverslide is the symbol of Big Hole haymaking. I have seen one or two in the Salmon River Valley and in Contact and Deeth, Nevada. But those beaverslides were built on location by Big Hole men. In the Big Hole they abound. Were it not for the Bitterroot and Pioneer mountains and the massive stacks themselves, beaverslides would dominate the landscape.

Russ pulls up in his four-wheel-drive pickup and says, "Wanta ride up to the Ajax?" The Ajax is one of the first ranches ever built in the Big Hole, a place I had long heard about and never expected to see. I did not know that the Petersons had bought it in the forties. We stop by the elk pen for a moment, where Russ demonstrates how to call elk. He shakes a bucket with some grain pellets in it and yells "Elk! Elk! Hey Elk!" An old rancher's joke. A cow and a young bull saunter up, and Russ shakes the bull's rack through the fence, something he does every day during the rut. Then we hop in the pickup, drive past the main house, out onto 278, and cut west again on a dirt road a couple of miles north. Next thing I know we are climbing a grade and scouting the beaver swamp below us for moose.

4

I HAVE NOT HEARD many farmers rhapsodize about machines, except perhaps for ones they used during childhood—two-cylinder Deere tractors or one of the early Farmalls. I was just old enough in the late nineteen-fifties to be brought to a final threshing in Lyon County, Iowa, the kind of event famous for many mouths at the dinner table, many piles of potatoes, many steaks. I remember nothing more about it than a windbreak of pines, a broken well-pump, and a deserted farmstead where the threshing took place. For a long time the threshing machine they used that day lived on my Uncle Everon's farm in a special shed, where I once collided with it on a Farmall B. The last time I visited—a year ago in June—it lay down by the old cowlane, along a fence where once a colt was killed when lightning hit the wires. I never heard a farmer rhapsodize about animals, either; closest to it came Louie, when he said, "I prefer livestock."

He made that observation late one afternoon after he and Reggie and I had fed the cattle in his lower feedlot. We hauled buckets of ground corn down a concrete feed bunk while the sun fell through the trees lining the Rock River, and when we were done we stood at the end of the feed bunk, watching the cattle eat and listening to them snort when the ground corn stuck to their wet noses. Louie reached down and pulled up a dark green rounded stem growing beside an ancient silage wagon. He ran a thumbnail up the stem, splitting it open so that Reggie and I could look inside. We saw the young head of a grass still, as they say, in boot, wrapped in the plant's outer sheath. Louie said, "Oats." Behind us the steers drooled and the pigs clanked their self-feeders and ran about in high heels while we looked at the afternoon past an old metal sign that marked the far end of the bottom feedlot to which the floods had risen last spring.

If farmers were at all disposed to rhapsody, they might get eloquent about the work itself, and particularly about the process of adaptation. There is a machine for every job on the farm, and yet much of the work, it seems, falls between machines. Figuring out what to do with a sickle blade that will not fit is the appointed labor of farming just as surely as is planting oats or combining soybeans. The Unexpected stalks a farm in big boots like a vagrant bent on havoc.

Not every farmer is an inventor, but the good ones

have the seeds of invention within them. Economy and efficiency move their relentless tinkering, and yet the real motive often seems to be aesthetic. The mind that first designed a cutter bar is not far different from the mind that can take the intractable steel of an outsized sickle blade and make it hum in the end. The question is how to reduce the simplicity that constitutes a problem ("It's simple; it's broke.") to the greater simplicity that constitutes a solution.

Louie is gifted with land, gifted with good hands, head, partner, and the measure of brute strength required for sound farming. He is not completely comfortable, however, when forced to tinker with the minute tolerances of an internal combustion engine, and because he does not take on certain kinds of jobs himself, there are gaps in his tool collection. Not to mistake, though. When, in the heat of the day, the windrower rattles and dies on the south slope of the alfalfa field, Louie has its guts out in no time and concludes that the problem lies in the carburetor's needle and seat. But actually to fix the needle and seat, his first recourse is to his neighbor, Harlan Kessler, who is at work on his IH 1066's air-conditioning. All sorts of problems go down the road to Kessler's, among them Louie's sickle blade.

Harlan's place lies two miles south of the Logers, and it is marked, if you arrive from that direction, by a huge dead tree, bleached white as a cast antler. To the north, a dark and forbidding wood cushions the farmstead from prevailing winds, a wood where the Red-Cross Knight might have found himself "wrapt in *Errours* endlesse traine." Within the grove, a flock of sheep wanders, one of the last in the area. (There are

more mink than sheep in Rock County, Minnesota.)
The flock has denuded the soil and stripped the trees as
high as sheep's lips can. The earth has turned gray from
sheep. Downed timber lies exposed, unrotting, like
driftwood, instead of breaking down rapidly into pith
and fungus.

The trees have their revenge, though. The earth in
the grove is so parched and overbitten that it will no
longer support the flock, and Harlan, who buys little
sheep chow, is forced to let the flock graze on his lawn
and along his steep ditches. The sheep wander freely
onto the road, and many are struck by cars. In four visits
to Harlan Kessler, Louie and I saw three casualties: two
lambs and a ewe, to which Harlan's comment was, "There
goes the profit margin." Like the trees, they too lay
exposed, unrotting, on the gravel near the chickenhouse,
where a line of tractors waited for repair. Visiting Harlan's I began to understand my father's longtime dislike
of sheep, which dates from his boyhood sheepkeeping
days ten miles south of here.

Harlan is no farmer. What the deedbooks and any
local will tell you is that the Kessler farmstead is un-
connected by ownership or rental with the fertile land
lying around it. Harlan is a mechanic. He tells the season
by the machines that appear in his shop. He has a youth-
ful, aquiline look, smooth-faced, pale, and fully fleshed,
and he wears an International Harvester cap stained with
sweat and every liquid a machine can exude. Next to
Louie, who is deeply tanned and wears a red Kent Feed
cap from the Kanaranzi Elevator and a graying, early
Solzhenitsyn beard that leaves his long upper lip clean,
it is obvious that though Kessler lives in the country he

belongs to the caste of small-town mechanic and body-shop owner. He runs the kind of business that enthralls townboys, and not for the tool-supply calendar girls alone.

The two ugliest dogs on earth, one walleyed and bald-pated, the other disposed to bark from the prone position, nose around our ankles. They offer no grace to repeat customers. The mangy one bit a seven-year-old girl in the face, and visitors, recognizing the threat in its ugliness, know not to shove it away with a boot. Farther back in the yard, Harlan's son pitches a ball against the barn; he does this on every visit we make. He wears an old-fashioned, roundhead baseball cap and shiny dungarees. Young Kessler looks like a miniature Christy Mathewson. He rocks and throws with the regularity of a preternaturally shy pro. The *thwock* of the ball follows us into the shop. Harlan's only comment on his son is: "Boy don't know what a battery cable looks like."

When Harlan talks he has a Minnesota drawl that lingers over the word "swather" almost as though it were pronounced "lather." "Swather giving you problems, huh?" He and Louie chaff as work gets done, and they chaff over the pickup door when it is time to leave. They have a shared joke whose theme is largely the fact that they are both droll men, wry in humor, dry in tongue. The joke's punchline seems to be that it requires no words. A stranger picks it up from the way they greet each other, as if they had spoken on the phone just a minute before and knew perfectly well who had had the last laugh. It comes from living two miles down the same road and from the frequency of visits back and forth. When a post-hole digger at Louie's is missing, he knows without being told that Harlan hitched it up while we were out in the field.

Louie's plan was to bolt one of the heads from an old sickle blade, which he knew fit properly, in place of the head on the new sickle blade. To do so, he needed to reinforce the old head, weld its bolt holes shut, and cut new holes to fit the spacing of bolts on the RazorCat. Harlan got the job because Harlan has a better drill press and welding gear. This was mere blacksmith's work for Harlan, who is accustomed to boring and grinding engine metal to thousandths-of-inch tolerances. But then he gets a lot of less than exacting work from his customers.

ONE FINE DAY after the alfalfa was cut, Louie, who sits on Clinton Township's board of supervisors, and I drove to Steen, where the township stores its road machinery, to bring Harlan some custom. The township maintains gravel roads and field access drives. The county keeps up county roads and the farmers mow the ditches, unless they support Pheasants Forever (a hunters' conservation group), in which case they spot spray and receive a cash award. The ditches get mowed not for neatness but to keep down the cocklebur and bull thistle.

The road to Steen from Louie's crosses the gravel flats west of the Rock River, just north of the Iowa border, and edges the hamlet of Ash Creek. Ash Creek reminds you that economic crisis in the Midwest is nothing new. Back, as Louie says, "before my time," a train line called the Bonny Doon stretched from Doon, Iowa, to Luverne, Minnesota, a run of perhaps thirty miles. That passenger train turned Ash Creek into a significant depot in the early twenties when it had a bank, general store, blacksmith, grain elevator, and, most important of all, a dancehall. When the Bonny Doon ended service, the Ash Creek depot wilted. The village is laid out now like a broken comb, rundown houses next to vacant lots. Its frontyards fill with children, its backyards with downed machinery of a uniformly rusty color. Porches are glazed with plastic sheeting. Whatever the Bonny Doon brought to Ash Creek, it took away again when it left. Ash Creek is "welfare," a word Janelle and Louie pronounce with some disgust.

Steen is also a hamlet—a cluster of neat houses to which, over the years, farmers have retired. Like a circle of musk oxen, the houses in town have their backs to the fields. At the center, instead of oxen young, there is little more than open space filled sparsely by Clinton Township's quonset hut, a defunct Golden Sun feed store in a decayed stucco building, and a body shop, where a young man was rebuilding—almost from scratch—a 1928 Model A with soft top and rumble seat. The township's $500-a-month hired man met us beside the township's $150,000 Champion roadgrader, which they had too little snow to use the winter they bought it. (It got a workout in late fall and early winter, 1985, when cold weather and snow caught the region short of #1 diesel fuel and corn was left standing in the fields.) The hired man, who looks to be sixty, has a single front tooth, and lives with his mother. He diverts himself with high-school basketball, popcorn, and beer.

The township's ancient Allis-Chalmers, which the

38

hired man uses to mow the ditches of dilatory farmers (who are then charged for the service), needs transmission work. It tends to pop out of gear at disconcerting moments. For that it will go to Harlan's. The immediate problem is that it will not start. So we visit the young man building the Model A in hopes he will have a battery charger. His father does, and after some friendly visiting about the virtues of Model As, whose dependability was recognized by an early, superior, and departed breed of mailman, we get the tractor started. The Allis is so old that it has a positive instead of a negative ground, which causes some tongue clucking. In third gear, Louie retraces our route through Ash Creek, which does not gain on one at eight miles an hour, and across the Rock River while I tail him, lugging, in his white GMC pickup. On the low ground west of the river, the grass in the ditches grows thick and high, and meadowlarks lean from the fenceposts and sing. Here and there, a couple of horses are tied up in the bromegrass along the gravel's edge.

When we drove into Harlan's with the Allis-Chalmers, the Kessler women were in the yard. On the house side of the drive, across from the shop, they were washing a car. The oldest of the three was dressed in a full black skirt. In another neighborhood, she would have sat in front of a tenement and tatted lace. The two younger women—high-school age—stopped work and gawked as we pulled in. One wore short denim cutoffs and a T-shirt, the other a tight bright turquoise bathing suit, which made her dark complexion shine. Both were heavy and moony, and they hosed down the hood and flopped a rag across the roof with a kind of shy curiosity barely distinguishable from shamelessness. They paused again to stare as Louie and I pulled out of the drive toward home, past dark-eyed sheep nibbling on the corner fence.

BY THE MORNING of the VFW dance, the sickle blade was ready. After fitting it to the windrower, we timed the sickle drive. A sickle blade has only a three- or four-inch stroke, so its triangular knives must intersect perfectly with the guards that hold the blade in place, otherwise the windrower loses much of its cutting power. The guards prevent the alfalfa from bending away from the knives. (It was the combination of knives and finger guards that made Obed Hussey's nineteenth-century reaper a better machine than Cyrus McCormick's initial device, which tried to duplicate the action of a pair of scissors.) After a half hour of hand-cranking the sickle drive, measuring the gap between blades and guards, and loosening and tightening the pivot bolts, we finally got it right. By this time a small group of spectators, all of whom would be doing the polka in ten hours, had gathered from breakfast.

Louie started the windrower and pulled it onto the gravel driveway between the house and shop, the header still raised two feet off the ground. He climbed down and carried a five-gallon bucket of used motor oil out of the shop. Dipping it with a bent quart oil can, he poured black goop over the sickle blade, winked smiling at one of the spectators and said, "Aw, I got it dirty already." Then he climbed onto the seat and set the sickle blade and reel in motion. The blade slicked back and forth at more than a thousand strokes a minute. It sounded

like the mandibles of a plague of hoppers, wicked and remote from divinity, spitting oil instead of hopper juice. Louie regarded it with an air of satisfaction, as if this were the sound of earthly bliss, and took me for a ride.

I stood in what can only be called the forecastle of the windrower, a railed platform ahead of the driver, unintentionally designed to accommodate visiting nephews. From there I could lean directly over the header and scrutinize the machine at work. We waddled with a curious side-to-side motion down one of the rutted access roads that thread Louie's land. I got my sea legs and tried not to white-knuckle it. We bumped past the bunker silo, a huge pit dug into the side of the hill where the machine shop sits, and paused at the lowest edge of the alfalfa field, at the same level as the river bank, on a corner where alfalfa, cornfield, and feedlot meet. We headed due south.

Louie's alfalfa field is shaped like the state of Nebraska, if Nebraska were fourteen acres big, had square corners all around, and pointed north on its longest axis. Set into the Colorado notch is the hardwood grove east of the house. The field's complex topography undulates shallowly and then more deeply as one moves from north to south. A small flat, the only substantially level portion, runs from the northwest corner, where we were about to start windrowing, to the southwest corner. Complicating matters further, the field drops sharply from east to west, and a drainage course, which must be avoided for half its length, bisects it down the slope. Louie planned to cut a single swath, once around the field in a counterclockwise direction, just to see how the blade handled. The real cut would come during a stretch of good weather.

The rain had let up, but if anything the wind had stiffened. The alfalfa seemed not to wave or billow in the breeze so much as to abase itself voluntarily against the earth. Plants on the rises flattened themselves like men under fire and then sprang erect again. Noise from the exhaust stack behind us blew away and left us in silence or flew into our backs and warmed us. Louie lowered the header, engaged the drives, and we moved forward, the wicked sickle sound muffled, its teeth full of alfalfa at last.

Hanging over the machine like the figurehead of the good ship "Urban Boy," I peered into the header below me. Stiff ranks of alfalfa shuddered slightly under the impact of the sickle blade and fell straight back onto the conveyer belts. They bounced toward the center gap like almonds on a sorting line and disappeared. I turned around and looked back over Louie's head. A narrow swath of crushed alfalfa emerged from the tail of the machine and pointed straight north to four persons standing in a clump at the edge of the feedlot. They all waved briskly.

Louie did not simply chuck the machine into gear and head off down the crop line. He adjusted to lateral irregularities in field layout and to vertical ones as well. As we turned the southwest corner and began to angle uphill, the ground grew more rugged and Louie's hands and boots moved more rapidly. Several times he paused, backed off a hummock, changed the height of the header, and moved on. Other times a sudden wash of brown soil appeared at either end of the header and got sifted into the leguminous mix. I turned around in time to see a shaved crown of earth slide under the caster wheels at the rear. Twice Louie stopped the sickle drive, hopped down off the machine, and dislodged a clod that threatened to overpower the cutter bar. Louie yelled up at me through the racket, "Damn pocket gopher hills tear up the sickle." All the gophers in earshot were thinking just the opposite.

This trial run reminded me of an excerpt from the *London Daily News* in November 1851 quoted in John Steward's erudite history of the reaper. As part of the brisk competition for reaper sales, both Cyrus McCormick and Obed Hussey, a Quaker originally from Nantucket, took their machines to England for field trials. Hussey succeeded in exhibiting his reaper at Windsor before Prince Albert.

The spot selected was behind the statue of George III, at the end of the Long Walk, fern—of which there is an abundance in that locality—being the article on which the machine had to operate. . . After a brief delay, the gear being declared in order, on went the machine, drawn by two strong horses, and heedless of ruts and hillocks in its course, which was very rapid, bringing down everything it encountered cleanly and completely, including two or three slices of turf at least a foot long, and more than an inch thick . . . Indeed the work was not confined to the fern; a rabbit who was not accustomed to this species of interference was started and cruelly lacerated before he had time to escape.

Regally impressed, Prince Albert ordered two of Hussey's machines. "He then, after expressing his gratification, rode back to the game-keepers and resumed his gun. After he had left, the machine operated well upon some rushes."

Game in southwestern Minnesota, warned by the windrower's roar, is well accustomed to this species of interference and usually makes good its escape, though that night over coffee at Country Kitchen Elmore Jack told us about once having rescued a fawn lying in the path of his swather. Louie and I scared up no rabbits or pheasants or deer. Insects were not so lucky. As the windrower took to the field, the swallows that filled the barn eaves and the granary dormers took to the air ahead of us. For them the swather served as a huge mechanized beater on a driven insect shoot. They arched and plummeted in the breeze, taking moths and other winged insects right off the rotating reel. When the wind blew in our faces, the path behind us closed with swooping, diving birds, like the wake of a garbage scow being towed out to sea.

At three or four points on this trial round, Louie and I sickled into pockets of sweet, rich odor. The air suddenly seemed dense with scent, the more so for the drabness of the day. The smell of newmown hay is an agricultural talisman that survives in our language even though most of its speakers are now pent in populous cities far from "The smell of grain, or tedded grass, or kine,/Or Dairy." Alfalfa is not the antique hay crop of peasant Europe, but its odor is rich enough to compete with that of the freshly scythed mix of grasses in traditional hays. Mowing into those pockets of scent brought to mind long hours of vacation driving when, in the early sixties, my family came home to Iowa after fishing in Colorado. Sleep was disturbed only when we slowed for the Nebraska towns where they dehydrated alfalfa in great flamelit plants and the night filled with the overpowering heaviness of the crop. That this was only the odor of cattle feed seemed outrageous, then and now.

We windrowed to the north and cut a close shave around the drainage runoff that courses down through the field. In its upper stretch, just below Bruce's fenceline, the ground stays too moist for alfalfa and produces instead a luxuriant crop of foxtail barley, also called squirreltail grass, the most beautiful plant in fourteen acres. Even on a gray day the long spikes that form its sagging head break light into irridescent purples and greens. Louie's comment on foxtail barley was this: "Put cattle in a field with that stuff and they'd rather starve than eat." No wonder. It would taste like a mouthful of fiberglass spicules.

We rounded the corner by the corn dryers and

swooped down upon the small crowd that awaited our arrival: Janelle, wearing a blue sweatshirt and jeans, white hair the color of the clouds stacked above us; my brother John and his wife Jill, both tall and thin, underdressed for the cool weather settling in, and Reggie, laughing at the sight of her husband up on the platform beside his well-seasoned uncle, who, as farmers will, looked more natural in a machine seat then he did afoot on earth.

Janelle says Louie's name in a way that comes from living with a terse man, the last syllable pronounced halfway between a long and short *i*. It has infinite modulations.

"Louayee, how's it cut?"

"Louayee?"

"Cuts pretty good."

In fact, the windrower has broken three guards and several knives on one pass around the field. Janelle shakes her head at the perfidy of renegade sickle-blade companies that sell their product without adequate testing. In a week, after the first cut is done, the manufacturer will send out a rep to look things over. When he comes he will be wearing tailored bell-bottom jeans, cowboy boots, and a red Lacoste shirt tucked into his pants, which causes a slight turmoil of flesh at his waistline. He looks like he has arrived direct from a Kansas City convention for copy-shop owners. He will examine the sickle blade from top and bottom, hem and haw, and then admit to Janelle and Louie that the company has never actually had this type sickle blade on this model windrower, even though the box it was shipped in says "International Harvester 230" on the side. Then he will leave, escorted up the drive by Sam the dog. Eventually, another rep will return and make some adjustments, setting things right in time for the second cutting of hay in July.

For now, Louie pulls the windrower onto the drive, oils it again, and parks it in the old hipped building where he keeps his less frequently employed machinery. Then we have a cup of coffee and wait for the sun to come out. It takes four days.

5

WHILE WE WAITED, here are the things we did.

Chores twice every day. Standing with a feed wagon at the silo, waiting for it to fill with corn and sorghum silage for the cattle in the lower feedlot. Two bales of hay for the yearling calves. A half-bale for the young Simmenthal bull that Reggie named Nelson because it was purchased from the Rockefeller herd. Check the twenty-six calves and their mothers in the pasture that straddles the river. Milk for the wild kittens in the calf barn. Pork liver for their parents. Feed Sam the dog. Feed ourselves, and give ourselves coffee. (The pigs take care of themselves, day and night. Self-feeders.)

Preparing for chores, stand by the corn dryer as an

auger ships corn into the IH feed grinder, which turns it into a rough powder. A sign on the corn dryer says: "Work with safety line. Avoid center. Avoid flowing grain. Danger of suffocation." In Louie's boyhood, when flax was still grown in this region, men drowned in flax seed. When one of the belts on the feed grinder breaks, replace it.

Drive to Kanaranzi Elevator on Monday morning, when the temperature is forty degrees, to buy sorghum seed and the herbicide 2,4-D, which kills broadleaf plants by causing them to grow to death, and Banvel (three quarts of each to 200 gallons of water, about a half pint per acre). The elevator man has sold half of Louie's sorghum seed to someone else. Louie talks of a two-hour wait in line to dump beans at the elevator during harvest. Kanaranzi may be the only town, hardly a town, just a small herd of buildings, in the country whose bank was held up by men driving snowmobiles. They fled across open fields, ditched the machines, and escaped in a car. They were never caught.

On the IH 656 I spray the young beans, which requires a windless, rainless day. So does the rest of the county. I listen to KEW and KQAD on the radio. I shiver in the cold, except when I drive into the wind. I get the point of closed-cab tractors. I keep my eyes peeled for killdeer and yellow-headed blackbirds. Janelle and Louie begin cultivating corn. The cultivating goes on for three days. Louie drills sorghum in a small field north of the house where beans washed out.

We pay some visits. To my dad's next-older brother, Kenneth, and his wife, Frieda. Ken and Frieda are the only town dwellers among my dad's siblings. Ken runs the NAPA parts store in Rock Rapids. Behind it he garages an immense white Cadillac (1959). When my dad is in town he sits at Frieda's organ and plays "Danke Schön." Ken is a cheerful man who collects Jim Beam decanters. All the bourbon remains intact, sealed, except what gradually evaporates through the porcelain. Ken specializes in Jim Beam autos and trains. He showed me two shelves full of original Jim Beam boxes and receipts.

We visit my dad's oldest brother, Everon, who has just returned from China where he and the rest of his World War II Flying Tiger squadron revisited their old bases. The living room is filled with Chinese gifts. Everon was a Norden bombsight specialist and lives on the home place, where my father was raised, the farm I know best. With Esther, his wife, he has raised a flock of boys (seven) and a single girl, Donna.

Bruce and another neighbor, name of Gary, stop by and ask for our help moving calves. Louie hitches his trailer to the pickup and we head a couple of miles north. Bruce's Holstein calves have escaped and high-tailed it down the road to a deserted farmstead where Bruce and Gary have penned them in an old dairy yard. The house stands vacant, drapes sagging, but the farm buildings are filled with pigs. In coveralls and work-boots, Gary and Bruce wade deep into the thick green muck of the yard and work the cattle toward a gate— I work them away from the barn. It takes two trips to trailer them back where they belong. While we are at Bruce's we pick up Louie's other bull, a Limousin called (unofficially) Red Nuts. Red Nuts and Nelson will be put out to pasture with the heifers in July and next spring there will be a new crop of calves. For the moment, Red Nuts and Nelson engage in some chivalrous combat.

Stopped to see W. Ray, who is always called W. (pronounced *dub-ya*) Ray. Louie has run out of square-baled alfalfa for his calves and W. Ray has some extra. W. Ray has a high wheezing laugh that explodes out of nowhere. His dog Ginger has just killed a skunk. "Git, Ginger, git outta here. And I gotta spend the rest of the day with her"—then that big surprising laugh from a man with wire-rim glasses. W. Ray built a fine new ranch house within three feet of a two-story stucco house that is gradually falling in. It took seven years to finish the new house. When W. Ray decided to build it, he immediately lost interest in the old one. Louie says, "He used to make you walk right in with your shit boots on." W. Ray and I toss down bales of second-cut hay from the hayloft of the most cavernous, heavily timbered barn I have ever seen. W. Ray recommends leather gloves for slinging bales. W. Ray is the kind of man (say Louie and Janelle, who both get a bang out of him) who will borrow your feed wagon, haul it all the way to Ellsworth and back, and then, to repay you, take you out to the Magnolia Lounge Bar and Steak Restaurant in Magnolia and get angry if you don't order the most expensive item on the menu. The Magnolia Lounge Bar and Steak Restaurant, with its $6.95 filets, may be the best place to eat in all of Minnesota.

We fix fence. Down where the Rock River curves around the beanfield, some wires are down and we find, flashlights in hand, news on the TV, a couple of cows standing dumbly among the beans. They hup back over the fence. The next night Louie and I decide to do a little catfish angling down where the cattle leaped the fence. We take a lunch (it is 8:00 P.M.), a thermos, and some beef liver. We thread the liver onto hooks and sling them into the river with rods and reels I found behind the bar in the basement. We fish for ten minutes, then agree it is too damn cold for June and head back to the house. Louie wonders if I am the angler he has heard I am.

Neighbors stop by in the evening to order seed from Louie, who represents Jacques Seed. My parents' house in California is filled with Jacques Seed paraphernalia—pitchers, calendars, hats, vests—as well as pig paraphernalia. Janelle and Louie are pork boosters and a portion of profits on their hogs goes to the Pork Producers' Association for advertising.

We go to Harlan's to pick up Louie's IH 1066. We

go to Harlan's to pick up a short battery cable. We go to J & M in Luverne to pick up a battery for the township's Allis and some sisal baling twine from Dubuque. We also stop in at Mark Jacobson's Luverne International dealership so Louie can pick up the electronic monitor for his corn planter after a forty-four dollar repair. The monitor tells the tractor driver whether the planter is seeding the ground uniformly. Last spring it blew a transistor no bigger than a corn kernel and omitted every eighth row in one of the upper fields, which Louie had to fill in as best he could.

And every day we walk out to the alfalfa and kick the swath we cut on Saturday. It has not dried. Nothing has dried. For three days it is cloudy and cold. I mow the lawn and the grove and around the implements beside the granary. I pretend I am windrowing alfalfa. I take walks through the alfalfa with Sam the dog. I come to know alfalfa.

6

GRASS MADE FLESH, about to hit the road for Minnesota feedlots. Cattle-buying day at the Spokane Ranch. Not the way it used to be, when the Union Pacific ran a special train from Divide, Montana, to Columbus, Nebraska, for the ranchers of the Big Hole. In those days, they drove the herds to Divide, loaded them in cattle cars, then hoisted themselves into the special caboose the Union Pacific provided, not forgetting the cards and whiskey. Today, Henry the cattle buyer is on the ranch, having driven from Minnesota with several friends in a rented car. There is a timing problem. The truckers have not arrived. It is also Saturday and there is no way to verify the transfer of funds. Everybody makes a lot of jokes about Henry leaving his checkbook at home.

Actually, the last time I looked, a couple of Henry's truckers were pulled up in front of Fetty's Cafe in Wisdom, two and a half miles east of the Spokane Ranch and fourteen miles north of the Forty Bar. Like me, they were learning Fetty's code: help yourself, and everyone else, to coffee. Fetty has a bad limp and cannot make the pot move at the speed it needs, so everyone pours. Bunches of hands, and a couple of drivers, in double layers of coveralls and insulated caps and beaten cowboy hats sat around laughing into their eggs. One, named Rick, wearing a brown hat so dead it looked like wet flannel, walked behind the horseshoe counter where I sat and helped himself to coffee. It slopped over the rim of his cup and onto the floor. He pointed the pot at me and said, "You probably won't trust me after seeing me spill this all over the place." Then he filled my cup and everyone else's at the counter. As if icons of autumn only come from New England, Fetty had hung fold-out waffle-paper Indian corn beneath the Great Falls Select Beer clock.

Cattle-buying is an uneasy business in these days of low steer prices. Maybe it has always been an uneasy business. Vera Rutledge, with her husband Fred owner of the Spokane Ranch, put the paradox of cattle ranching to me succinctly. "We always butcher our own beef, but a couple of months back here we ran short and I had to buy two forequarters. They cost five hundred and eleven dollars. That's more than we get for an entire cow." She also explained her economy of scale. "It just doesn't pay me," she said, "to buy potatoes in less than the ton." Good reason, too. She sat fourteen for dinner that day, hired hands, cattle buyers, husband, son, and visitor, who among them ate nearly a ten-pound sack of boiled Idahos. The cook was on vacation.

The only sign of uneasiness during mid-morning coffee is that no one wants to get too serious. Henry is not really worried about the condition of the cattle; Fred Rutledge is not really concerned about the transfer of funds because he trusts Henry. Jerry Rutledge, Fred's son, is a little anxious about the condition of a couple of water-bellied steers and he wants Doc, the "vetinary" (as everyone calls him), to take a look at them. Doc, like the brand-checker, is here ex officio, one of the parties required to examine the cattle before they are shipped. Meanwhile, Fred is teaching Henry's boys, friends who have come along just for the ride, how to win at the slot machine in his basement. He keeps a plastic margarine tub of quarters on top so no one will have to lose his own change.

Henry's friends are from Minnesota—Cannon Falls to be exact, near where Fred's cattle will settle in for one long last meal of grain and supplement. They look agricultural, all right, but not Montanan. They say things like, "Gee, this is some country, isn't it?" This has nothing to do with their being from Minnesota, more to do perhaps with being stunned by the drive and the giant-size hospitality of the Big Hole. They make short work of Vera's instant coffee and a plate full of fruitcake and cheese. Vera coaxes food upon them from the full kitchen in the basement. There is one upstairs, too. And a cook-house, of course.

After a while, with an air of nonchalance, Fred and Jerry and Henry and Doc head upstairs to Fred's office. They do some sober dickering over figures, and during the discussion, a decimal point gets misplaced. Three of the four men run private calculations in hopes of finding it, and eventually they do. The big question then is not how much but when. "I should have those trucks in here this afternoon," says Henry. "Tomorrow morning at the latest." The arrival of the trucks will be followed by many hours of steers grunting and squalling and shiftily walking the gangplank.

Fred Rutledge is a dark-complexioned, round-faced man who keeps a light burning in his eyes at all times. Talk long enough to people who know the Big Hole and you will eventually hear a couple of Fred Rutledge stories. Their quality depends upon the narrator. The one I like best I heard from Ray Ditterline, an alfalfa specialist at Montana State University in Bozeman. Ray is himself a pretty colorful character with silver side-burns and coachman-brown bell bottoms. When he has occasion to explain that a milliliter of water holds 10^9 rhizobia of the type that fix nitrogen on the root systems of alfalfa he says, "That's a whole slug of bugs."

Fred was driving Ray and a county agent from Dillon around Spokane Ranch one day, checking out a couple of experimental alfalfa plots, the only ones in the Big Hole. At one point the agent hopped out of the truck to open a gate that looked like it was about to fall off its pins. From the pickup Fred yelled, "You be careful, now. I got a hundred and one miles of fence on this ranch, and that gate there holds it all together." I suspect this is a line all ranchers with wobbly gates have uttered. It gets attributed to Fred because Fred has that kind of humor.

His son, Jerry, has it too, in spades. Partly it is the effect of talking, like his father, with a mouth full of chew, which causes an ironic biting off of words. (It

also makes two dark flecks of tobacco gather at the corners of his mouth.) It is a genuine, unmitigated pleasure to hear him talk, as much for the way the words come out half-gnawed as for what he says. He and his father are fine, shrewd men with disarming tongues.

Coffee breaks up and the gloves and cowboy galoshes come on. The cowdogs, bright mutts and blue heelers, leap into the back of one pickup and head off to the cattle yards. Jerry and I walk around the front to take a look at a couple of square bales of grass/alfalfa mix bound with orange twine. As Ray Ditterline said, "Fred's got some neighbors looking over his fences. He's buying a lot of new equipment." Not all of which works out. They have baled a little alfalfa on the test plots but mainly stick to oldfashioned stacks of wild hay. They tried a Hesston stacker too—a machine that makes huge loaves of hay—but it was too slow. At Spokane Ranch, oddly, experimental alfalfa grows best on top of some strange mounds. A visiting geologist told Fred they were formed by prehistoric gophers. Prehistoric gophers are the kind of pests the Spokane Ranch would have.

The Rutledges get strangers looking over their fences, too, mainly to see Vera's pet elk in a compound by Highway 43. Pickups pull over and drivers gawk at the bugling bulls. It is almost a public service; out of state hunters learn to identify their prey. In the field behind the cookhouse, Vera also runs a small herd of buffalo. Talk to anyone who knows the Big Hole well and you will hear Vera Rutledge stories too, like the one about the gelded mule deer that used to be a house pet, despite the white carpets.

Jerry and I met Doc down at a small steer pen. The two of them walked through the herd, singling out three waterbellied steers. They ran them into a chute that forces cattle to move single file and locked the first one into a handling cage, rendering the animal immobile. These steers have developed urinary obstructions that cause them to retain their urine. Hence they are water-bellied, or as Jerry put it, "all swole up full of piss." Tail-wringing is a sure sign of a waterbellied steer.

From the back of his four-door, which has a ply-wood floorboard instead of a seat, Doc pulled a plastic bucket and a satchel of supplies. CB chatter crackled from the dash. Doc tied the steer's tail to a rack. After donning a sleeve-length glove, he gave the steer a rectal exam and administered an anesthetic between the ver-tebrae just above the tail. He inserted the needle first and then attached the syringe. While he mixed an an-tiseptic in the brown plastic bucket, Doc, a country-banker kind of man, looked at me and asked, "Ever see one of these operations before?" I had not. Since a steer, to qualify for steerhood, has already been castrated, I wanted to learn the meaning of the verb "to heifer," as in, "We're gonna have to heifer that steer," or in its participial form, "How many heifered steers in this load?" Jerry shot me a quick glance.

Just to the left and below the steer's tail, Doc snipped away the hair and scrubbed down the area with anti-septic. Then he incised a slit about three inches long. The steer shifted its weight slightly. With two fingers, Doc reached inside the incision, grabbed the steer's ure-thra, and began pulling. He tugged mightily, breathing hard with exertion. At last its full length popped out, penis and all, two and a half feet of urethra. Doc looked it over carefully and held up the end two inches. "Here's the problem. It's rotten." He cut off all but the last five inches closest to the bladder. All around us the October snow was starting again. I noticed a Cat and a beaverslide and a couple of wheelrakes east of the cattleyard. The cowdog on the ground gnawed, growling, on a stick he had been carrying around for the last half hour. Jerry let a small gob of chew explore the consequences of gravity.

Doc tucked the tag end of urethra through the slit near the cow's anus and stitched the slit shut. From now on, in all but internal organs, this steer was functionally a heifer—that is, a cow that pisses from the rear. Jerry said, "Something, ain't it. First they cut off your balls and then they keep on digging." He suggested that having seen a heifering, I might want to look up Don and Bill, who were moving a haystack out in the fresh air. That sounded pretty good to me. Jerry muscled the second steer into the handling cage. As I walked away I heard him say, "See, Doc, it's pushed his asshole all out."

UNLIKE A MIDWESTERN alfalfa field, which has been trimmed and manicured for ninety years or so, a Big Hole haymeadow has ruts and rises, not to mention shallow irrigation ditches. Alfalfa is planted in soil, within limits the finer the better, but wild hay grows from the plain unvarnished ground. A haymeadow has foxholes and skunkholes and snakeholes and squirrelholes. It also has low spots that bog down and make it hard for a tractor and haywagon to reach the stack. So the stack moves to higher, firmer terrain.

Don and Bill are setting up to do that just now. A John Deere 4640 with Cozy Cab idles on one side of the stack, while a 1978 D8 Cat idles in deep echo on the other. Hitched to the Deere is a stackmover, either the first or the third one built in the valley, since the Petersons at Forty Bar Ranch own the second. Beaverslide baskets are usually twenty feet across, so stackmover wheels lie twenty feet apart on a rigid front frame. Fifteen welded-steel tines, each about twenty feet long, reach backward from the front frame. A crankstart gas engine sits in the center of the front frame; it generates just enough power to run two sets of hydraulics. The first hydraulic system loosens and tightens the half-inch steel cables that get wrapped around the stack. The second hydraulic system raises the entire front frame as much as eight inches off the ground, just to give the stack a little clearance in the front. The rear end always drags.

Don climbs into the Deere's Cozy Cab and backs the stackmover tight against the stack. Bill and I climb into the D8. The Cat's blade extends straight in front of us. Bill sets the Cat against the stack and then shoves it onto the stackmover's steel-tined platform. Most days Don and Bill can move eight or nine stacks. Things have not been going well this morning, largely because the ground is wet, which increases the friction between the earth and the twenty-five-ton haymound squatting on it. They knocked the top off the last stack they moved. When the stack is loaded, they unwind the half-inch steel cables from the front of the mover, wrap them around the stack, where they join with ring and hook, and cinch them up hydraulically. The cables disappear in the stack's soft belly. The Deere unhitches, and the Cat comes around and hitches up. Bill climbs down from the Cat and raises the front end of the stack. Then we are off.

It is an exhilarating ride. The wind has strengthened and the sky is no longer letting fall pellets of snow but ticket stubs of wet stuff. A glossy black skunk scurries from our path and dives down a hole. Bill occasionally works the hand clutch and the steering rods and the brakes in a glassed-in cab littered with tools. (A haystack doesn't need a lot of steering; it naturally seeks a straight line.) He wears ragged coveralls and a flap-eared hat and he is suffering from a cold, which has given him a bright red nose. I look behind us. Tons of hay, green where the surface has been scraped, straw-colored over the rest of it, tail us. With the six-cylinder diesel roaring, we easily break a landspeed record for grass mountains.

At our destination, four hundred yards away, waits Don, a taciturn, square-faced man wearing a trooper's hat and deerskin mittens. Bill pulls the stack directly alongside the line of stacks they have already formed. Don releases the tension on the cables, unhooks them from the stackmover, and hooks their opposite ends to the Deere, with which he pulls them free of the stack. Bill slips the stackmover out from under the hay and hauls it clear. Then he edges the Cat against the stack's open side, raises the blade again, and shoves it into the line. Bill climbs down and checks the oil on the Cat while Don, in search of a grease zerk, scrapes one of the Cat's hubs. This has taken an hour and a half.

Wild hay does not seem to mind Caterpillars and loaded stackmovers running back and forth over its surface. It comes up just as lush next spring.

THE TWIN-OVEN Wolf stove on which Dale, Jerry's wife, is making a farm pond of gravy will bake twenty loaves of bread at once. Vera hands me a hot slice, buttering it for me the way mothers do for children not yet promoted to knives. Dale says, "That won't be too good. I put in too much wheat flour." This merits no comment. The Wolf is a gas stove. I mention that Russ Peterson's mom still cooks over wood. "Don't we wish this was a wood stove," says Dale. I ask how come. Vera looks at me over the cream she is whipping. "Cooks better."

Vera is slim, short, and wiry, with a slightly bow-legged walk and an active face. Dale stands half again as tall and twice as thick. They are both as practical as jumper cables, brisk and good-humored. For dinner (lunch in all urban time zones) Vera and Dale have made two roasts, peas, two immense bowls of halved, boiled potatoes, the farm pond of gravy, a large serving dish full of cottage cheese, all the condiments for and enough bread to sop up the former, and plates of sponge cake covered with berries and whipped cream that is almost too fresh for tastes weaned on modern packaging. (They still milk at the Spokane Ranch.) Also iced tea and coffee.

Noon has come and no one has arrived in the dining room of the cookhouse because the National League playoffs are on TV. Jerry, hatless, comes in through the back door and carves the roasts. He slices off quarter-inch rounds and every now and then a sliver for himself and a couple for me. Dale says, "Where are those men? They'd never be late if cook was here," reaches up above the ventilator hood, and pulls a rope, causing a bell to clang outdoors. Jerry arranges the beef on a platter with his thumb, and then he looks at me and winks. "I guess I washed up some. How about you?"

There is a general shedding of hats and coveralls when the men finally show a couple of minutes later. All sit except Vera and Dale, who keep the food moving. Jerry introduces some of the hired hands to the Minnesota crowd as the Hole Brothers. They all have brightly scrubbed faces, and I hardly recognize Bill, who turns out to be a well-fleshed man, almost fat, something his coveralls hid. Everybody joshes him, until he looks up from the potatoes and says, "You gotta be a man to wear my suspenders." The hands eat quietly, listening sharply, but not saying much. Talk turns to the erratic weather. Henry asks if there's any way to gauge the onset of hard winter here. Fred grins and says, "There's only two kinds of people try to predict Big Hole weather: strangers and fools."

One of the hands tells a story about a family up in the northernmost stretch of the Big Hole. "Snow gets so bad up there in the wintertime the kids take correspondence courses instead of going to school. After a while they get skittish enough they need to be broke before company comes." By this time the sponge cake is going down, and the faster hands are starting to slip out of their seats. Jerry and Fred sit back from the table with Henry a little longer to talk about cattle. Jerry explains that the herd has just held weight over the last couple of days, maybe lost some. Henry says, "They look fine to me." Fred points out that they've had some hard weather to endure, so it's no wonder they're off their feed. "Fifty-five one day, then a soaking rain, then it dropped to zero and we had wind and snow the next day." Jerry says "I'm going to tell you one little thing —them cows appear to have lost weight. They look a bit gant."

7

DRIVE THE GALLATIN CANYON in snow often enough and it will happen to you. You come around a curve into one of the shade patches and there is a cattle truck lying on its side, wheels still spinning. Oil runs with the snow-melt in the asphalt grooves. Shit and straw have been flung onto the snowbank and cattle are lowing in plain-song desperation. "In Passing May We Urge You To Try Miller's Blue Ribbon Beef." That is what the tail-gate says.

In front of the cab, a bearded man from a VW van (which he rolled in the canyon the day before) has pulled the driver through the windshield, laid him out on tow-els, put a space blanket over him, and filled a plastic litter bag with snow to make an ice-pack, which he holds to the driver's cut and bleeding head. A small young nut-brown woman with no teeth in the top of her mouth has been drawn by curiosity from another car. She looks at the driver and says, "Poor man." Then she wiggles her ass as if she were settling onto a cold toilet seat: "And I gotta pee so baaaad!"

The driver of the lead truck for Miller's Blue Ribbon Beef (coveralls, long red nose) runs back to help. But there is nothing to do. The cattle cannot be freed from the trailer until more help comes. Shit and straw cover their flanks; somehow most have regained their footing but not their composure. A high-school kid on his way to football practice arrives. A wrangler from the kid's father's ranch passes the other way. He arranges to bring some men and stock and corral the cattle back against the canyon wall. The wrecker pulls up seconds later. A man in a long bushy moustache gets out and starts breaking up the cluster of cars that have stopped. He has already radioed ambulance and police.

An angry young woman in a Toyota Supra wheels over and starts shooting photos of the event with a camera equipped with telephoto lens and motor drive. She is the head of a local committee to ban semis from the Gallatin Canyon, and she makes an angry speech to the small group of good citizens gathered around the hurt driver.

And there it is: wrapped up and docketed in a matter of moments.

There is nothing to do. You pass a sheriff's car on your way south and he waves, headed toward the accident. You stop at the Park Entrance and ask two rangers if their Park Service Suburban would do as an ambulance. They're already on the horn about it. Just inside the Entrance, a flock of ravens is having a heavy lunch of dead elk.

There are seven steers waiting for them up the road.

8

AS IF TO MAKE some private point about means and ends, God gave kine four stomachs and a diet of hay, and he made them chew each mouthful twice. To man he gave a single stomach and an indiscriminate palate, but he made him take his alfalfa as pre-macerated pellets or plastic-coffined tussocks of sprouts. Man seems omnivorous until you consider the things he can't digest, like tender oak-leaf shoots or lime-green lichen or sweet-smelling greenchop. It's one of those facts of life: if you want to eat alfalfa baled in early bloom, you have to be built like a fermentation vat on hooves.

A modern cow is a mobile energy conversion factory. Whether bred for lactation, weight gain, or sexual reproduction, its capacities and potentials have been calculated to the nth degree by ag schools and the federal government. In recent bovine literature, the cow seems no more creaturely than a solar panel or a heat-exchanger. Except on one point. Cattle actually like alfalfa—that is, they express a preference for it, a preference stronger than a solar panel's love of a sunny day. Amid punctilious calculations of alfalfa's nutritional value, scientists toss their pencils in the air and say, "Alfalfa apparently possesses some peculiar property to stimulate appetite or satisfy the taste buds when cattle have been on high concentrate rations for two or three months." But they are not sure. There is a problem: "Because the animal cannot tell the observer whether it does or does not eat a forage for a sensory reason . . . the word [palatability] holds some ambiguity." Such is the nature of agricultural research in a world where cows can't talk.

De gustibus non est disputandum, especially in the feed-lot. Farmers and ranchers have been so eager to satisfy their finicky herds that annually they grow twenty-seven million acres—seventy-five million tons—of alfalfa in the United States (though who knows what they would do if cows could talk and expressed a preference for, say, Antarctic krill or twinkie cake.) The majority of that alfalfa sees the light of day on small fields like Louie's in the upper Corn Belt, and the majority of that is harvested in bale form, though an increasing percentage is fed as greenchop (fresh, chopped alfalfa) or haylage (slightly wilted, chopped alfalfa). Cows like the Queen of Legumes standing, lying, chopped, shredded, stacked, baled, dehydrated, and cubed. They don't much mind her moldy.

One man, George Clothier, tried to voice barnyard sentiment on the subject of alfalfa. Writing in the first decade of this century during a rapid expansion of acreage devoted to alfalfa, Clothier sounded the unmistakable note of agricultural evangelism. "The alfalfa plant," he wrote, "furnishes the protein to construct and repair the brains of statesmen. It builds up the muscles and bones of the war-horse, and gives its rider sinews of iron. Alfalfa makes the hens cackle and the turkeys gobble. It induces the pigs to squeal and grunt with satisfaction." I imagine Clothier, surrounded by resentful children, sitting down to alfalfa bisque at lunch.

Walking through a field of alfalfa you would not suspect you were in the company of a miracle plant. As farm crops go, alfalfa is an unruly one, not given to synchronous billowing like oats or wheat, not regimental in rank like corn. From a single slightly subsoil crown, several slender-branched stems protrude at angles often well off the vertical. From those branches shoot oblong trifoliolate leaves that arch through a hundred and forty degrees during the day to follow the sun. In early bloom, just before cutting, an alfalfa field looks like a closed canopy of green leaves, two and a half feet tall, mottled by purple flowers. After cutting, it is a miscellaneous gathering of shrub stumps with bare earth between.

As far as beauty afield is concerned, alfalfa has the disadvantage of being a perennial, the only perennial grown regularly by midwestern farmers. Each spring a newly planted field of corn spears out of the earth like hope itself, subject only to the tyranny of the summer to come. Alfalfa is a sadder but wiser plant. It has borne the harshness of winter past. On the north slopes of Louie's alfalfa field the prevailing wind blew away the snow cover during the winter and some ice-sheeting killed several patches of alfalfa. The field has bald spots, irregularities. But then alfalfa is also a more provident plant than corn. When hot weather comes and the rains fail, corn turns to newsprint; alfalfa simply grows dormant and waits for thunderheads.

The asymmetries in an alfalfa field stem partly from the way the crop is seeded. It is laid down regularly enough—Louie uses a grain drill—but it doesn't come up regularly. "It's a crap shoot, a numbers game," said Ray Ditterline in his office at Montana State. "Here in Montana we use seven pounds of pure live seed per acre. That works out to thirty seeds per square foot on irrigated land. Half of those emerge. That's fifteen. Thirty-three percent of those are resistant to a bunch of diseases and insects, which leaves five plants per square foot. In Montana, you need four plants per square foot for maximum yield." The raw numbers are different in Minnesota (normally Louie uses ten pounds of seed per acre), and the percentages are slightly better, but Louie can expect only twenty to fifty percent of his seeds to mature and survive the first winter. Here, again, corn has the edge. Corn has big seeds (you know, kernels) which, as Ray says, "come piling out of the ground." Companies like DeKalb and Pioneer and Jacques sell corn seeds eighty thousand to the bag (which will plant four acres for Louie) irrespective of weight. A standard fifty-pound bag—enough for five acres—contains two and a quarter million alfalfa seeds. Approximately.

When Louie first sows a field with alfalfa he also

plants with it a nurse crop, oats, which is nurselike only to people who consider Florence Nightingale a malign influence in medical history. Oats in an alfalfa field (unlike, say, "volunteer" corn in a beanfield) is an intentional enemy. Alfalfa seedlings—instead of fighting weeds all summer long—compete for light and nourishment with the oat seedlings until Louie decides the contest in alfalfa's favor by harvesting the oats. Then the alfalfa is on its own for three years—cut and baled three times each summer—until Louie plows it under and plants that effervescent bounder, corn, on its grave.

As fall comes on and hard frost threatens, alfalfa stores carbohydrates in its crown and taproot. (One reason alfalfa doesn't mind a little drought is that its taproot can reach as deep as nine meters into the earth.) Energy that would have gone for leaf and stem growth gets conserved. When I asked Ray Ditterline about this after an October snow in Bozeman, he leaned back in his desk chair, coffee in hand, and said, "Alfalfa's just like a big ole bear gittin ready to hibernate—or like me," slapping his gut and laughing. A grizzly is in big trouble if she cannot forage heavily before hibernation, and alfalfa suffers if it's cut too late in the season and can't build up its energy reserves. And, too, a grizzly may not make it through the winter if the snows don't drift deep and heavy over her den. Same for alfalfa, which needs insulation.

When spring comes, the plant seeks a new equilibrium. It burns its crown and root reserves until young leaf growth provides enough energy through photosynthesis to begin harboring carbohydrates again. The plant puts out buds and leaves and begins to think about showing its five-petalled flowers—what botanists call, in allusion to its butterfly shape, "the papilionaceous corolla." Alfalfa flowers consist of a large upright banner, wing petals on either side, and two lower petals fused together to form a "keel." No sooner do delicate purple blossoms appear than, sunny weather come at last, Louie will drive his IH 230 with the new blade into the field and sickle all the plants within four inches of their lives. It is the end of May, start of June.

Fortunately, cutting is not the crisis it appears to be; alfalfa does not despond. It simply acts as if spring were come again. New secondary stems, sprouted from crown buds, begin to grow alongside the main stem. The plant again depletes its energy reserves as it waits for enough leaf growth to begin carbohydrate storage. By the fourth of July it flourishes again, and again Louie cuts it. The cycle recurs, and in mid–August Louie makes hay a third time. In effect, he has forced the plant to choose vegetative instead of reproductive growth. It never gets to bear seed.

This, besides being a perennial, sets alfalfa apart from the rest of the major midwestern crops: it is the only one not cultivated for its seed. (Alfalfa seed production is a specialized industry centered mainly in the western states.) Seeds—grains and kernels—are themselves a form of low-moisture energy storage, and as a result they stockpile well. This leads, by some technocratic logic, to farm surpluses, federal grain elevators, and eventually price supports, planting restrictions, and PIK programs. Every year the county extension agent hands Louie a list of allowable acreage limits for corn, oats, and soybeans. Nowhere does the list mention alfalfa. There are no federal bale barns, haylage hampers, or greenchop price supports. Alfalfa is an *ad libitum* crop; only cattle know how much is enough.

When I say that Louie bales three times a summer, I make it sound too simple. In fact, haymaking is the most weather-threatened operation he undertakes all year long. Harvest creates new heroes. Corn will tough out terrible weather in late October and November. As long as combines and cornpickers can get into the fields without miring to their hubs, the crop can be salvaged. Alfalfa is as delicate after cutting as it was stalwart beforehand. It demands two or three low-humidity, windy, sunny days before it is ripe for baling. (Providential wisdom is not kidding when it says, "Make hay while the sun shines." In baling weather you think you will live forever.) At Janelle and Louie's we waited for a cold front (Thursday's storm and the next four days) to blow through before we windrowed, because a cold front carries haymaking weather behind it. When the rain stopped, the sun shone and the breezes blew, and Louie's rows of windrowed alfalfa, cut on the first bright noon, gradually turned light green. The foxtail barley, where we had clipped too close to the drainage course, turned silver.

As I WALKED THROUGH the alfalfa, watching it dry to the baling point, inspecting the damp green on the underside of the windrows, I found it possible to believe that the genetic substance of seeds is the genuine stuff of human culture. That is an old idea, one every plant breeder knows, but it takes some grasping. It means that a direct line of culturing (or as Milton would have said, "manuring"—working with hands) descends from alfalfa's proximate source, eaten millennia since by a primeval grazer, to Janelle and Louie's field. I am used to the kind of culture whose antiquity can be found looking ancient in manuscripts and codices and books, in the shifts of language. If I could see an antique alfalfa plant alive, it would not be figured in majuscule script or Baskerville type. It would look like an ancient constellation of molecules coming up (today!) on an oceanic plain in Minnesota, cut, drying, waiting to have its leaves bound.

TECHNICALLY, ALFALFA IS called *Medicago sativa*, and it belongs to the *Leguminosae*, the second largest seed-bearing family of plants on earth. You will recognize soybeans and peanuts and clover and kudzu as its siblings. (As a family, legumes have the honor of appearing in a Thai dig dated about 9000 B.C., "the earliest archeological evidence of vegeculture.") Like most cultivated plants, alfalfa was the object of human care long before recorded history, particularly among cultures in the region of Persia (the Iranian plateau) and those who traded with them. Alfalfa is a Persian native, accustomed to the short dry summers and cold winters of northwestern Iran, where there are neutral, calcareous soils with good drainage. Though greater climatic flexibility has recently been bred into the plant, these are still its basic demands.

Medicago sativa first entered the archives about 1300 B.C., when a Hittite inscribed on a brick tablet the news that alfalfa was a nutritious winter feed for livestock.

The gardener of a Babylonian king mentioned it in 700 B.C. under the Iranian name *aspasti*, which means, not surprisingly, "horse fodder." Not much later, the Greeks discovered alfalfa through war, the usual conduit, in this case against the Persians. They called it *medike*, to indicate its Median origin. (The Median Empire, essentially Iran and Cappadocia, became part of Persia under Cyrus in the sixth century B.C.) Like most things Greek, it passed to the Romans, who expressed a technical genius when it came to forage plants. To them it was *medica*.

The Romans—including Virgil, Varro, Pliny, and Columella—discussed it thoroughly, displaying as much knowledge of alfalfa as anyone would have for another eighteen centuries. They spread the plant to southern Spain and Switzerland. (Islam later carried it farther into Europe.) Then the Roman Empire collapsed, and as if it were a Platonic text known to the Greeks but not to the Franks, alfalfa was not heard of again for nearly a millennium. It re-entered cultivation in Lombardy during the twelfth century, but only with the late Renaissance did alfalfa return to widespread cultivation in the rest of Europe.

By 1720, alfalfa had appeared in England, where, as in most of Europe, it was (and still is) called "lucerne," probably after the Swiss region around Lucerne Lake. (Where alfalfa is called alfalfa, it has been introduced through Arab influence, particularly out of Moorish Spain, for the word derives from *alfacfacah*, which means "the best kind of fodder.") In England lucerne, like sainfoin, another legume, attracted the interest mainly of "scientific" farmers and the gentry because it required far more care than conventional fodder. Nurse crops and, of course, herbicides had not yet entered the repertoire of alfalfa growers. The only alternative was intensive cultivation.

In his "Rural Ride" for 29 September 1826, William Cobbett, one of the great agricultural reformers, described the prevalent English system for raising lucerne. He also gave a pretty clear picture of its value.

> Mr. Walter Palmer's lucerne is on the Tullian plan; that is, it is in rows at four feet distance from each other; so that you plough between as often as you please, and thus, together with a little hand weeding between the plants, keep the ground, at all times, clear of weeds and grass. Mr. Palmer says that his acre (and he has no more) has kept two horses all the summer; and he seems to complain that it has done no more. Indeed! A stout horse will eat much more than a fatting ox. This grass will fat any ox or sheep; and would not Mr. Palmer like to have ten acres of land that would fat a score of oxen? They would do this if they were managed well. But is it *nothing* to keep a team of four horses, for five months in the year, on the produce of two acres of land? If a man say that, he must, of course, be eagerly looking forward to another world; for nothing will satisfy him in this.

By the middle of the eighteenth century, alfalfa had passed to the community of learned farmers in America, but it did not meet with notable success. In 1795, George Washington and Thomas Jefferson exchanged letters on the subject. "I gave the Lucerne," Jefferson wrote in mid-September, "a good coat of dung, and due tillage;

yet it is such poor dwindling stuff that I have abandoned it." A month later Washington responded: "Lucerne has not succeeded better with me than with you; but I will give it another, and a fairer trial before it is abandoned altogether." Their experience was typical of most eastern farmers who experimented with alfalfa. It took yet another route of origin, from Spain via South America to California in the mid-nineteenth century (which explains why Americans call lucerne alfalfa), to bring about the successful introduction of alfalfa in this country. From central California, it spread rapidly to neighboring states, to the Mormons in Utah, and eastward into Kansas. The only apparent limitation to its range was the brutal winters of the north central United States. Rock County, Minnesota, for instance.

WASHINGTON AND JEFFERSON failed as makers of alfalfa hay because the soils they tilled were too acidic. Had they limed the fields before planting, they might have succeeded. But they also failed because they were ignorant—as everyone was until 1886—that the history of alfalfa is also the history of a bacterium, *Rhizobium meliloti*. As D. K. Barnes, an eminent alfalfa breeder, writes, the link between alfalfa and *Rhizobium meliloti* "is essentially a host:pathogen association. In this association the plant provides an energy source and a suitable environment for the bacteria, while the bacteria provide a source of usable nitrogen for the plant." Sow *Medicago sativa* where *Rhizobium meliloti* is absent and you get "poor dwindling stuff" indeed, bonsai alfalfa.

Rhizobia are microsymbionts with two interesting

attributes, infectivity and effectivity. The first measures how readily they infect a host plant, the second how effectively they convert gaseous dinitrogen, N_2, a form of nitrogen that alfalfa cannot use, into ammonia, NH_3, which it can. Microsymbionts for legumes are species specific; *Bradrhizobium japonicum* will infect soybeans and peanuts, but not alfalfa, while *Rhizobium loti* will infect lupines and chickpeas. Moreover, different strains of *Rhizobium meliloti* fix nitrogen in different varieties of alfalfa with differing degrees of effectiveness.

Once infected, an alfalfa plant develops nodules, like a bubonic plague victim's buboes, on the root hairs that protrude from the taproot. (Bacteria infect only one to five percent of the root hairs.) Before nodulation takes place, there is love, so to speak, in the rhizosphere as "elicitor and receptor compounds" on root hair and bacteria bring about "mutual recognition by the partners." After this moment of discovery, the root hairs curl (invitingly?) and *Rhizobium meliloti* penetrates the plant. Then there is a brief epithalamium. To quote D. K. Barnes again, "after penetration, infection threads develop through which the bacteria migrate to the root cortex." There, through cell division, a nodule containing bacteroid tissue is constructed. Up to this point, the bacterium has been the aggressor, but gradually a genuinely symbiotic, stable relationship is formed.

Healthy, elongated nodules produce an enzyme called nitrogenase, which fixes dinitrogen. N_2-fixing nodules are pink or red in their centers, the tint created by a protein called leghemoglobin—related to human hemoglobin—which neither plant nor bacteria can produce alone. In the bacteroids, the symbionts convert gaseous dinitrogen to ammonia, which is then transformed into alpha amino compounds and consumed by the plant. As a nodule ceases to fix nitrogen effectively it turns from red to green as its protein content changes. This process too follows a cycle. N_2-fixation slows in the fall and stays sluggish in the spring, but during summer's growth it picks up tremendously. After cutting, bacteroids die off, reducing N_2-fixation, only to be replaced as new plant growth begins. *Rhizobium meliloti*, like *Medicago sativa*, responds vigorously to well-scheduled, routine harvesting.

N_2-fixing is not just a neat bacterial trick, a pseudo-erotic, subterranean sleight of hand. The cost of farming varies, of course, with the price of land and machinery, but it depends directly on the price of petroleum products. Chief among them is fertilizer, mainly nitrogen applied in the form of anhydrous ammonia. Nitrogen is what field crops consume from the soil in bulk, ten million metric tons of it annually, a million metric tons more than farmers apply as fertilizer. It is "the major limiting nutrient for production of corn, small grains, and for more than 81 million hectares [two hundred million acres] of grassland in humid areas of the U.S." Unlike most crops (even soybeans, which, as Ray Ditterline says, are "shitty N_2-fixers") alfalfa not only brings its own nitrogen to lunch, it leaves leftovers. This is something Columella knew in 60 A.D.

Usually, an abiding rhizobial community persists after a field has been planted to alfalfa, even following rotation of other crops. But where rhizobia are not present, farmers must introduce it by inoculating the seeds. This used to be a sloppy, hasty process. Rhizobia are light-sensitive, so in a dark barn farmers mixed a bacterial slurry, usually with a sticky base of some kind. Some recommended water and molasses, some water and sugar, some even Coca Cola. The inoculated seeds were set out to dry in darkness, then dumped in a grain drill (which clogged with sticky seed) and planted immediately while rhizobia perished left and right. Today, the seeds come with an inoculant coating and a guaranteed shelf life. One milliliter of water, Ray Ditterline repeats, contains ten billion *Rhizobia meliloti.* How many in a fifty-pound bag of pre-inoculated seeds? A whole slug of bugs.

Modern alfalfa research has mainly been dedicated to varietal adaptation, the most important of which overcame alfalfa's native climatic limitations. Wendelin Grimm, a German immigrant, brought to Minnesota in 1857 twenty pounds of a Franconian hybrid of alfalfa produced by crossing *Medicago sativa* with *Medicago falcata*, a hardy, yellow-flowered species of alfalfa whose range extended into Siberia. (Grimm's Franconian seed had resulted from natural hybridization occurring in northern France and Germany as early as the sixteenth century.) Grimm planted and cold weather selected until together they created a genuinely winter-hardy alfalfa. Since Grimm's day, breeders have developed varieties of alfalfa resistant to such major diseases as bacterial wilt, to stem nematodes, and to significant insect pests. Louie—directly indebted to Wendelin Grimm's Minnesota research—uses Jacques 90R.

EARLY JUNE, JUST before cutting, and a biotic diapason plays in the fourteen-acre field beyond the corn dryers.

In the deep, black soil laid by centuries of prairie grasses, Indian brushfires, and buffalo grazing, alfalfa taproots soak up the water of Thursday's storm, surrendering far less topsoil to the Rock River than the neighboring corn does. Root hairs absorb potassium until they indulge in what agronomists call luxury consumption. Nodules distill ammonia from the raw earth and send it stemward. Leaves stiffen with protein (up to a quarter of their dry matter), and bees begin to trip the keels of the few purple blossoms showing, exposing anthers and stigma and carrying away nectar and pollen.

The time is ripe for a cut, and Louie makes it. The crushed alfalfa still respires in the windrow, even as it begins to dry. Its moisture rises when the dew falls and diminishes in the afternoon heat. Should it rain while the alfalfa is on the ground, nutrients will leach away like badly set dye. But we are lucky. We get three drying days in a row. The crimped stems are moist, but the leaves, still full of protein, have become almost brittle, likely to break off and be lost if handled too roughly or too much. Louie pulls the Vermeer round baler out of the machine shop. Grease gun in hand, he finds the Vermeer's hidden grease zerks and pumps them full. He loads the twine bin on the side of the machine and ties the balls of sisal twine together. Then he rolls the Vermeer onto the field behind the IH 1066 (air-conditioner on) and makes hay. From a distance, as the baler ejects a bale, Louie looks like the brain of a heavy-carapaced, ovipositing insect that came to earth this splendid day in a small field of alfalfa stubble just north of the Iowa border.

9

WHEN RUSS PETERSON daydreams about getting away
from it all, he means "a cabin up in the quaking aspen."
(The stress falls heavily on the first syllable of "quaking.") He hasn't cut the logs yet, but he knows a site
just inside the treeline west of the Ajax. You guess the
kind of place it is by listening when Russ, not a wistful
man, stands at the edge of Twin Lakes and says, "At
night the mackinaw in that stream between the lakes
spawned so loud it woke us up." Up in the quaking
aspen he will raise a cabin between the sound of mackinaw and the wind in the leaves.

The Forest Service has graveled a new road to Twin
Lakes that cuts around the Ajax. Like most new Forest

Service roads in boggy terrain, it looks like a low, gravel-topped levee. Russ, Shirley, and I take a private track to the Ajax that forces us to choose between high ground lofty enough for a microwave relay ("That's the phone," said Russ) and low ground. Only the latter leads to the Ajax, twisting through terrain that Forest Service maps mark with five-fronded swamp symbols. We run the high road for half a mile. Russ is draining the acres below us. The bronze swampwater takes naturally to the ditch he and his sons have cut. Down there the ground, a peat bog, quakes like the aspen. It quivers under the print of moose.

Before we backtrack to the low road, we stop to look at the country. A brown arm of cottonwoods reaches around the far side of the swamp, red with willow and silver with beaverponds under a cloudy sky. Beyond lie haymeadows and pastures rising gradually to a narrow sagebrush bench and the treeline of the Bitterroot range. Sheep Mountain, Pyramid Peak, Ajax Peak, and Squaw Mountain, from which Slag-a-Melt Creek runs, lie above us, a dark blanket of trees mottled by the undercoat of snow. Scattered bands of cattle flank the road and dot the willow-hemmed patches of open ground. This year's green and last year's tawny haystacks halt north and east of the swamp. Across the valley, the highway to Dillon has been folded into the hills, invisible.

Driving past the bog, we break out of willows into a huge paddock, parallel the edge of it, then break through cottonwoods or aspen or willow and into another paddock again and again. We pass knee-high gray wooden boxes that keep the cattle's salt supplement from dissolving on the moist earth. The truck thumps over

shallow irrigation ditches that run north and south perpendicular to the slope of the land. Russ says, "We
figured out soon enough that if you want to water a
haymeadow you run the ditch across the top of it instead
of through the middle. That way the water soaks all the
way down the field. Otherwise you get a half-watered
meadow."

Irrigation makes the light soils on these bench lands
bear hay. Water abounds in the Big Hole and cattlemen
who drove stock into the valley in the 1870s could count
on finding riverbottom grass sustained by spring and
summer flooding. But to winter cattle and live year-round
in the Big Hole, river hay was not enough. You had to
bring water to the benches. Frank Stanchfield, who has
a modest ranch and guiding operation near Wise River
and is a descendant of one of the Big Hole's first settlers,
described how this was done. It was July, and as he
spoke, he pointed to a shelf of green grass well above
the Big Hole River, which slows behind a V-dam just
upstream of Frank's place. At his feet, Mark the fat
beagle and a wry blueheeler sported. "My dad, who is
eighty-three," Frank said, "cut a long ditch from the
Wise River over to those fields up there with a fresno
and a horse team. That was all sagebrush in those days.
Give it enough water and sagebrush grows itself to death,
so the irrigation killed it off. Then they went in with
pulaskis and ripped out the stumps by hand. Every year
they pulled out a little more sage and planted a little
more grass. They hand broadcast the seed."

Ranchers entertain several theories about killing
sagebrush, or rather several theories about killing sagebrush entertain ranchers. Water works well, though some

claim it drowns the brush and others, like Frank, say it causes it to spend itself growing. Some folks use chemicals. Others burn it off, which also does the job. The one thing you don't do, said Russ, is try to plow it under. On the way up to the Ajax he showed me a plot of sagebrush he had plowed when he was too young to know any better. If you were looking for a field of high-yield *Artemisia tridentata*, you found it: the mother lode.

In the 1880s, when permanent settlers first entered the Big Hole, killing sagebrush and cutting irrigation ditches was still a labor of years. That explains why the oldest ranches sit right down in the river and creek bottoms near marshy ground. The price settlers paid in mosquitoes they saved in ready hay. One of the two Ajaxes lies low like the rest of the Big Hole's early ranches. The other rises high. The low Ajax is a ranch purchased in the forties by the Petersons, once owned by Will Montgomery, and before him by Alva Noyes who bought it from C. E. Stanchfield. Until the teens of this century, the high Ajax was a working mine originally called the "Carrie Leonard" and located at the head of Big Swamp Creek about ten miles (as the crow flies) southwest of the Ajax Ranch and more than half a mile up the Bitterroots. From the mouth of its main shaft at 9,750 feet above sea level, the Ajax's turn-of-the-century owner, Alva Noyes, could look out of Montana and down into Idaho's Salmon Valley.

Noyes had a weird faith in the Big Hole Basin. He built a dirt-roofed house in it and settled for good, angering ranchers in the Horse Prairie (the next valley south) who were accustomed to using the Big Hole as free summer range. Noyes remained philosophical. "The stockman is always very selfish," he wrote in *The Story of Ajax*. "It is part of his business to be." Despite his willingness to affront Horse Prairie cattlemen, Noyes did not really have his heart in ranching in the Big Hole. "I did not believe that money could be made in running stock cattle at such a high altitude, as too many calves would be apt to perish from cold at birth." So he turned to one of the ways you reportedly could make money at high altitudes in the West: gold-mining.

His chance came when an old prospector named Frank Brown gave an interest in a mining claim to Mrs. Noyes, "a little slip of a girl in short dresses" when Noyes married her—so little a slip, in fact, that her father went to court to prevent the marriage. (Hattie Noyes also owned the four hundred acres of "desert land" that became the townsite of Wisdom. Apparently she matured into a heady woman.) Around 1894 Noyes bought the Ajax Ranch from an Indiana man who held the mortgage from C. E. Stanchfield. With three partners he also bought the Ajax Mine.

First assay reports from the main shaft on Ajax Peak looked good. Noyes and his partners cut a road to the Ajax and began to meet the bounders in the mining business, about one of whom Noyes writes, "As a gas factory he would have proved an immense success." They bought a stamp mill for crushing ore and dug new shafts and shored them with timber. They built an arastra and talked about running a tramway to the mine. The first shipment of ore off the mountain weighed two hundred and ninety-nine tons. It yielded twenty ounces of gold, three hundred and forty-one dollars worth. Noyes, a poet about the profits of mining, felt keen disappointment. Later ore shipments proved only slightly more profitable, leaving the partners short of capital to develop the mine. Noyes visited Boston in hopes of selling Ajax shares only to discover that the market for speculative mining shares was glutted. The public had grown cynical about western gold ventures. In May 1907, to begin covering his debts, he sold "the Heart" of the Ajax Ranch—nearly three square miles of the lower end—to Will Montgomery for eleven dollars an acre.

SHIRLEY UNLOCKED THE gate to the Ajax and tossed a Coors Silver Bullet can she had found on the dirt track into the back of the pickup. Like all deserted ranches and farmsteads, the Ajax was a melancholy place. Until a dozen years ago, the Petersons had lived here, but a dozen years of bitter winter and heavy snow will pull apart almost any structure. The larger the building, the more it had suffered. The log house was wind-torn, sinking on its foundation in the soft earth. A timber dairy barn had withstood the elements more ably, but it too seemed chapped and weather-smooth. Russ and Shirley looked about them with great fondness at a thing they could not prevent happening. Russ recalled having, when he was a boy, to rope pregnant cows and drag them into the dairy barn to calve. "If I didn't kill the cow or the calf or myself, we might get along."

Apart from the absence of corrugated steel sheds and green propane tanks and the presence of dumbly proprietary cows in place of horses, the Ajax did not look any more antique than the Forty Bar. Russ said they hayed the meadows that lay around it when they lived at the Ajax, but now, so far from the Forty Bar and its long congregation of haystacks, the meadows had become open pasture. Standing amid the grasses of one meadow, snow eddying gently, I realized that part of the Petersons' continuity with the past lay in the look of the land around them. I had almost expected to see the Ajax as it might appear in a gum print or a deep-bordered etching or through a silver-nitrate haze. Instead, the obvious occurred to me, the way it sometimes will. At this time of year in Alva and Hattie Noyes's day the meadows looked exactly as they did at that moment. The grass was brown, the willows were red, the aspens rustled, and the snow, even in October, promised to fall forever.

Life in the Big Hole has gotten lonely enough, the way Wisdom and Jackson have shrunk, without living six miles through bog and pasture off the main highway. The Petersons used the snowplane only on special days (Pat said you froze to death in it), and Russ's new Cadillac Seville would high-center a hundred times on the Ajax road. There were lots of good reasons and almost no bad ones for moving down to the Forty Bar, away from the heavy timber above the Ajax. These are not the kinds of decisions an outsider can question. When you come from beyond the Big Hole anyway, you wish for a chance to live in either place, Ajax or Forty Bar. It makes no difference.

ALONG A FENCELINE by the barn lay a pair of old horse-drawn Case mowers, the kind whose gears and wooden pitmans and blades were driven by the rotation of their iron-cleated wheels. They had turned the same color as the cottonwoods. Towering over them stood a much newer, but older-looking beaverslide, made entirely from peeled logs. Like the mowers, house, barn, outbuildings, and Ajax entire, the beaverslide had fallen out of service, replaced by the steel-reinforced one at the Forty Bar. It looked like half the skeleton of a quadrangular teepee or a massive Indian travois with a Coney Island batting-cage set under its angle. No analogies do a beaverslide justice.

Like all harvesting, haymaking is merely organization, the rule for which seems to be "store in the most voluminous package possible." In the Big Hole, volumes are immense. If you set out to make a haystack using conventional agricultural implements, the height of the stack rapidly outscales them and you confront the fundamental problem of haystack building—getting the hay on top of an ever-growing pile. You could bring the crane the boys are using on the new bridge into the field and make a stack with that, but it would be slow and ridiculously expensive.

Early solutions to this quandary included the Mormon derrick, nothing more than a huge bipod with a sling attached. The sling lifted the hay and the bipod tilted to drop the load of hay on a stack much taller than a man, but shorter than the derrick. Unc showed me photos of Mormon derricks at work in the Big Hole in the 1890s. They looked like gangly, inefficient hay tools in constant danger of toppling.

The same year Alva Noyes sold the Ajax, two Big Hole ranchers, Herb Armitage and David Stephens, built a stacker that was nothing more than an inclined plane, much like a giant, stationary version of the wheeled hay loaders used in the East between the 1870s and 1930s. But where the hay loader had a series of revolving belts and forks (powered by ground drive) which pulled hay up the incline and into a wagon, Armitage and Stephens' device had a single wide basket, made of protruding wooden tines. Buckrakes loaded hay in the basket at the bottom and a horse team pulled it up the incline by cables run through pulleys. The basket dumped the hay over the top to form a stack.

When the machine was patented in 1910, its inventors called it the Beaverhead County Slide Stacker, a name rapidly conflated to beaverslide. The etymology of beaverslide hardly matters; it has been abandoned to the assumption that the hay tool has something to do with the animal. I sat one night in the Petersons' house and talked with Rich Shepherd, who makes beaverslides in Jackson, and his wife Shirley, a square-jawed, forthright woman. "I don't know," said Rich, a florid young man who was off to steelhead in Idaho the next day, "I always thought it had something to do with beavers, like a slide beavers would make." Pat said, "Maybe a slide out of their lodge." This sounded reasonable to all of us, though I suspect that an inclined plane named after a form of animal egress might better have been called an otterslide.

I asked Rich about the new steel-reinforced beaverslides he was building. A fire burned under a mantelpiece lined with ceramic cowboys, and Pat carried in coffee from the kitchen. Along the far wall hung a print of cattle-feeding in winter—draft horses pulling a haysled, men and animals clouding the air with their breath. A pair of recliners, a long couch, and a loveseat filled the north end of the living room. Rich leaned back on the couch, coffee on his knee, and talked briefly about the machines, which were refined in Kenno Krause's shop (also in Jackson) and then in his own.

"It's twenty feet up the slide to the drop and then probably another twenty, twenty-five feet to the top of the derrick. [Derrick is simply another name for beaverslide.] Most beaverslides are twenty, twenty-one feet across." Inclined to quietness, Rich stopped talking. I asked him how much the new beaverslides cost. "About ten thousand dollars." How long do they last? "Forever." He smiled as he said this.

"That depends on who's running the hoist," Russ

said. "You get somebody who bangs the basket against the top every time and no beaverslide is going to last very long." He recalled one day when they had hooked the hoist cable that raises the basket to a Caterpillar just to hold the basket in place while they were doing repairs. The Cat driver forgot why he was sitting still and drove away. Before he realized his mistake he had smashed the basket over the top. "We got one neighbor here"—Russ laughed—"who really bangs away at his derrick. You go out along the fenceline and you can hear that basket crash into the top every time he raises it." Haying crews put the senior man, the man with touch and good coordination, on the hoist. He has a hand brake, a gas pedal, a gear shift, a clutch, and the responsibility if the whole thing goes.

LAKE CREEK RAN dark from the peat. After I closed and locked the gate to the Ajax, Russ, Shirley, and I parked on the bridge and looked down into the water for signs of fish. There were only peat-hued gurglings from below. Russ began to tell me the Pynchonlike story of Cowbone Lake, which Shirley had also told me. In November 1906, Russ's father, Sam, trailed six hundred head of cattle into the Big Hole from Salmon, Idaho. They had ridden up the Lemhi Valley, up Pratt Creek, and over Goldstone Pass, on their way to the trail down Darkhorse Creek and into Jackson. Just north of Goldstone Pass, the herd stopped for water at the edge of a frozen lake. Sixty of the cattle lurched onto the ice and fell through. The story ends with Indians wintering on the margin of Cowbone Lake and living off the carcasses.

That is an article of Peterson family history, one they are glad to tell because on a good map you can still find Cowbone Lake just north of Goldstone Pass. You can't help wondering if Sam Peterson would take kindly to preserving the memory of that day. He would probably display the emotion, recalling those shrieking cattle and confusion in the rest of the herd, that Russ did when he talked, visibly moved, about a bad season in the early seventies. A disease called scours, which causes fatal diarrhea in calves, had spread up and down the Big Hole, ranch to ranch. "A calf would be born in the morning, perfectly healthy it looked like," he said, "and by nightfall it'd be dead. It was enough to drive a man crazy." The Petersons lost seventy percent of their calves that year. "There was nothing to do but pile the bodies up and wait for the gutwagon," Pat added. That is a story they tell only once.

Russ and Shirley and I drove off the bridge and back over the track we had taken to the Ajax. Afternoon light, clinging to the land, seemed to flee to the snowy sky as twilight drew on. The Big Hole gradually lost its scale and attained the intimacy of a small alpine pasture where mountains shoulder in on the open. In the first darkness on the western slope behind us lay the Ajax and Ajax Mine and peat bog and now-quiet cattle. Ahead of us where light still hung, it all somehow came down to Darlene's cookhouse, where steaks, green beans, home fries, fresh-baked bread, salad, gooseberry jam, and applesauce cake awaited us.

But as we broke through another hedgerow of willow, Russ paused and Shirley reached across his arm and switched off the ignition. Ahead of us, a lean bull moose had flushed a fat cow moose from her cover. She galloped smoothly across the pasture, stopping now and then as the bull struggled not to lose ground in the chase. Midpasture, he locked his knees to catch his breath. The cow looked over her shoulder at the bull, peered past her bulbous nose at a white pickup in the distance, and took off down the line of browse in search of better genes.

10

IF IN 1961 YOU walked out the south-facing porch door
with an aluminum K in its latticework past the lilacs
and across the yard, you came to a dairy barn on Everon's farm. On one side were milking stalls. Holsteins
entered from the west, had suction milkers attached to
their udders, and clapped down a steep concrete ramp
to the south when they were dry. Across from the milkers was an undivided room for calves and their mothers
who would soon enter the production line. At the end
of the central corridor was a simple ladder, boards nailed
to studs, rising through a trap door in the floor of the
hayloft. From the south door of the hayloft you could
see the dairy yard and the beginnings of the lane, a stately

colonnade of elms, leading down to the school–corner pasture. A small stream ran through it during the wet. You could also see the windmill in the pasture and hear it creaking.

If you walked east along the fencing from the front of the dairy barn, you passed a cowtank, always slightly scummed, and arrived at the steerbarn, a mysterious and also somehow uninteresting place. Feedlots full of fat-groaning steers stretched behind it. North of the steer-barn lay the pigs. They had a fenced–in yard to themselves where they gnawed their wooden feed troughs and ran coyly back and forth in the presence of humans. The hoghouse was a less comical place, full of farrowing sows as fat and neglectful of their brood as termite queens. North of the pigs stood the garage in the loft of which during Prohibition my grandfather made beer for hay-ing. Still north of that stood Esther's chicken coop and the chicken yard, a sunny, dusty place. Northernmost of all grew the grove, home of all intrigue and all terror for farmboys and townboys alike. Pullets had a house to themselves there.

Around all of this, dairy, steer, hog, and chicken yards, ran a confused region of vegetation, not yet field, not quite weed, bordering the tractor road that led to the crops themselves. (In 1961 Everon raised oats, soy-beans, corn, and alfalfa. His father raised a more diverse menu of flax, alfalfa, red clover and timothy, wheat, oats, and corn.) And around all of this, particularly on the farm's western edge, rested tractors and implements which, in 1961, still retained their human scale, even to a boy of nine.

Two farm words have always appealed to me. The

first is "section." The farm was the only place I knew where section, one of the most general words in English, had a specific meaning: 640 acres or 1/36th of a township. (Half-section and quarter-section are acceptable fractions. Smaller than that and you get into the eighty- and forty-acre fields.) As a boy I wanted to be able to say, "I'm so hungry I could eat a section of pecan pie," though I knew that whoever heard me would assume I had never learned the meaning of "piece."

(In Iowa last spring, my cousins Myron, Davis, and Randy plowed an entire section. They plowed from gravel road to gravel road without hitting the fencelines and pheasant cover that usually mark the halves and quarters. They also planted a thousand acres of beans, forty more than a section and a half.)

The other word is "yard." Farms have yard and lawn. Lawn is grass that goes bald under big trees. Yard is the public space—dirt except when mud—between house and barn, the agora where trucks, tractors, combines, and cornshellers convene. The elevator carrying bales to the hayloft on its chain conveyor protrudes into the yard. Ruts in yard-mud freeze solid in winter. At Everon's farm, the main yard lay between the lilacs and the dairy barn, an area big enough for two semis to play tag. A side-yard by the machine shop and chicken coop lay east of the house. Guests parked there unless they were staying less than half an hour; then they left their cars on the edge of the main yard nearest the porch with the aluminum door. A broken wire gate marked the border where yard met lawn and the two fought it out.

When, young, I spent a week or two on the farm alone, my parents arranged their departures in the yard.

101

The promise in that time was enormous, but then so was the loss. I was still in Iowa, surrounded by Klinkenborgs (who were surrounded by still more Klinkenborgs). Ahead of me lay the prospect of milking cows, making hay, throwing cobs at the hogs, and perhaps breaking an arm like my cousin Jim, who tried to do a tight-wire act across the hayloft on twine string (as they say on the farm). But eventually I would have to enter that strange house and watch the darkness settle outside. It had a coal cellar filled with corncobs and a wall of grease-stained overalls and a pair of staircases and a hundred bedrooms. The fracas of TV game shows and stories (as my Aunt Esther called soaps) filled it mornings until the men came in for dinner and naps. I found it hard to believe that here my grandparents had raised my dad, who drove west with my mom through a windbreak and then turned south toward George, leaving me with my cousins in the yard.

Davis and Jim and I slept upstairs in the end bedroom that overlooked the machine shop. Two things worried me when I first spent a week with my cousins: rumors of ringworm and an unnamed infection detected only by a minute black spot on the soles of one's foot. For some reason, it forced the sufferer to wear tube socks to bed. I did not want to return to my family with a malignant black spot on the foot or an ovoid redness reaching up into where hair should be like drought into a temperate zone.

The first morning I woke late to hens clucking over their feed and a tractor pulling a manure spreader through the yard. But quickly I caught on. Before light had properly swelled beyond the steer pens, my uncle shouted up the stairwell: "Davis! Jim! Myron! Get up! move it!" He pointedly excepted me from roll call, but I would snap awake anyway and begin trying to rouse Davis, who seemed completely dead to the threat in his father's voice.

In time I lost all fear of farm dangers and became a farm danger myself, oblivious to bulls and sows and belts and pulleys and hot manifolds and hydraulic lines and power take-offs. I even got to be some use when it came to things like carrying a pail of milk to the house or, eventually, pulling an empty hayrack with the B. But I never completely conquered awe of Everon, my father's oldest brother. I admired his size—six foot three like all his boys—and his exuberant language. My father, under extreme duress, once when I was young said "hell," but when he hangs around Everon these days the "shits" fly. This tells you more about my father, a teacher, than about Everon, a school-board member for years.

Once, I rode home from Grandma and Grandpa Klinkenborg's Sunday afternoon with Everon, Esther, and Davis in the family Chrysler. We had passed the point where the farm first becomes visible on the gravel road, and I had begun to feel more relaxed about leaving my parents, brothers, and sister behind. As we drove along the trees shading the lane that the dairy herd took to pasture, Everon's curiosity grew. The cattle were not in the pasture, nor were they in the lane, and it was not yet close to milking time. About thirty yards before the drive, he knew what had happened. The cows were in the corn. I did not actually see the cows in the corn. I saw Davis watching his father's eyes in the mirror and a strange look come into his own.

"Shit!" my uncle yelled. "Them damn cows are in the corn. When I catchem I'm gonna shove mud up their butts."

I didn't know whether this was a traditional curse for cows in the corn or not. But I thought it was tremendous. Davis giggled. So did Esther, who titters with main force.

"You think it's funny, huh? Well, you're gonna help me catchem. Shit!"

Ever after, when Everon stood in the stairwell and shouted "Davis! Jim! Myron! Get up! Move it!" I expected him to add, "or I'll shove mud up your butts." Eventually that came to seem no more fearsome a threat than ringworm, which I never got.

WHEN YOU HAVE a big brood of sons and daughters, haymaking comes easy. One of the boys will be a wrestler and he relishes swinging bales on the hayrack. His brother, too young for high school, will emulate him. One of the girls will be a precise driver, missing barely an alfalfa stem as she steers up and down the windrows. While one crew works in the field, another tosses bales off the rack onto the elevator in the yard and another lifts them off the elevator and stacks them in the hayloft. Eight is a good number for haymaking with small square conventional bales: three in the field, one shuttling hayracks, two loading the elevator, and two stacking bales in the loft.

But when, like Janelle and Louie, one of your sons manages Butler Building outlets in Northern California and the other buys cosmetics for a midwestern department-store chain based in Green Bay, Wisconsin, haymaking is a trouble and a worry. You may get your Butler Buildings at cost and your atomizers free, but you will put up your hay with pain. Unless you own a round baler. What a round baler saves is labor; what a large family using a round baler indisputably loses is an intangible sense of community. The landscape loses something too. Instead of rickety yachts of hay with three-man crews running down the windrow, the horizon holds only a single heavy-carapaced, ovipositing insect.

Round balers do not produce spheres of hay any more than square balers produce cubes. One yields cylinders, and one yields fourteen by eighteen by thirty-six-inch rectangles. When round balers were first introduced in the late forties, they created narrow cylindrical bales meant to compete in size with sixty-pound square bales. Round-baled alfalfa in those days looked like a field full of hay-colored Sears, Roebuck sleeping bags. (Balers of that generation are still popular in parts of Missouri.) When round balers were reintroduced (more successfully) in the early seventies, they were designed to create "packages," as baler people say, weighing between a half and a full ton.

Even the unobservant noticed the mid-seventies shift from square to round bales. Fields were suddenly filled with huge biscuits of hay that eventually collected end to end in long lines and turned a dismal gray-brown. By March they looked as if farmers had settled on a convenient way of packaging waste: roll it up, line it up, and let it rot. But the appearance of rot was deceptive. If you no longer milk and your barn is not in trim, the hayloft may not withstand the weight of fourteen or fifteen acres of alfalfa (baled three times a summer) resting on its beams. You may not have a pole shed for storing bales. If you must expose hay to the elements, a simple ratio (the same that explains why elephants stay warmer than voles and why haystacks come so big in the Big Hole) prevails: the larger the "package" the smaller the ratio of surface area to volume. More hay rots on the surface of many little bales than rots on the surface of a single large one of equal weight.

A round baler looks like a towable cavity in a cage. It requires explanation. It does not seem possible to produce tight twelve-hundred-pound bales in an over-sized clothes dryer. I watched Louie's Vermeer at work, but I didn't understand the process until an engineer drew me a diagram. Like all balers, a round baler has a pickup, revolving tines that grab the "material" (be it alfalfa, pangola, sudan grass, corn stalks, or cane) and feed it into a small chamber. The alfalfa is forced against a wall of belts (or chains or rollers depending on the manufacturer) traveling upward at high speed. The belts carry the alfalfa vertically a short distance until gravity intervenes and causes it to tumble downward. It lands on top of more alfalfa being forced against the belts, and a cylindrical core of hay begins to build. Hay rises and falls on hay that is rising and falling. The core swells, pushing the belts back, until it fills the inner dimensions of the round baler. Farmers who use older round balers know a bale is finished when they get a crick in the neck from looking rearward. Newer balers, when the bale is done, sound an alarm or flash a light in the tractor cab.

With a full bale in the chamber, no more hay can be fed by the pickup, so the driver stops and waits while the baler ties and ejects the bale. A small tying arm scoots back and forth across the spinning bale, wrapping it in twine, and a blade razors it off. The driver backs up, a tailgate opens, and the bale emerges. If the driver has handled round balers much, it will be perfectly cylindrical, tight, and well-wrapped. If the driver has not yet learned to weave back and forth across the windrow, filling the ends of the baling chamber more than the center (which always takes care of itself), the bale will be humpy in the middle and inclined to looseness on the ends. Twine will feather in the breeze.

One reason farmers use windrowers is that the less alfalfa is handled the more of its leaves, filled with protein, it retains. Round balers are tough on alfalfa. They subject fragile, often brittle leaves to dryer-like agitation. Leaf loss can be high. Dairy farmers, whose cows need the finest hay to sustain milk production, do not use round bales. Beef men do. Louie stands his round bales on end in a rebar rack in the middle of the feedlot and leaves them to the discretion of steers.

THE OLD PASTURE at Everon's schoolhouse corner is now a cornfield with a drainage patch running through it. The windmill still stands, but its pipe is broken and it no longer pumps. Farmers on town water are part of a general pattern across the Midwest, like farmers on the electric in the thirties. If you look south from Louie's alfalfa field, the most prominent landmark is a water-pumping station, and from the schoolhouse corner at

Everon's you can see the single white digit of a rural water tower rising from a nearby hill. The windmills stand some places, but even when the vanes are not broken the pumps are dry. Most places they have been pulled down.

Old silos, tile or brick, have long been replaced by Harvestore silos, bunk silos, or no livestock at all. Cattle finishing is a risky operation, a gamble that many farmers will not take. Cattle also keep farmers home year-round, unlike cash crops. Dairy barns stand until they blow over in a high wind. Their foundations serve as dry platforms in the muddy season. Regulations have made it too costly to milk. Since corn is now combined, not picked on the cob, the old wire cribs that once lined the ditches near farmsteads are gone. My dad asked his nephew Randy if anyone picked in the cob anymore and Randy said, in his peculiar drawl, "Where they still got the good crib."

At Everon's in 1961, the farm was organized in concentric circles. Crops grew in the outermost ring. Then came a band of livestock and their barns, houses, and coops, then a yard of machines, and a nucleus of humans at the core. The nucleus still abides. Though her boys are grown and have houses (and in some cases wives) of their own, Esther feeds nearly as many for breakfast now as she did in 1961. The house has filled with man-size recliners in front of the news. But the periphery has lost interest. They stopped milking years before the dairy barn toppled. The hogs pork up in confinement systems on another place, steers nowhere to be seen. And no one raises chickens commercially anymore. They do what Myron's wife Mary does: keep a hundred broilers for friends and family. Unless they happen to be friend or family to Mary. Then they keep none.

The ring of animals and their barns, houses, and coops, the prime attraction to boys, has dispersed. In its place, resting on some of the same foundations, is a thicker and costlier ring of machinery. Where Esther's chickenhouse guarded the entrance to the grove there now looms a new corn dryer and storage bunk system, tubes and ladders arching over the top. It looks like a small Brazilian refinery. In the space two '61 tractors and a wagon would fill, an articulated International Harvester tractor hulks. It must bend at the waist as it turns ahead of a cultivator with wings that fold like the wings of a Navy jet.

SATURDAY, A WEEK after the VFW dance and another one only a day's work away, thirty-nine round bales lay in Louie's field. While Louie made hay for another neighbor, I did Janelle's job. I drove into the field on the IH 656 with a two-tine fork mounted on its three-point hitch. I backed the fork longways under a bale, lifted it off the ground to a cocked angle, and stored it back by Nelson the Simmenthal's and Red Nuts the Limousin's pen. I did that thirty-nine times. The sun shone and the radio played John Fogerty's "Centerfield" and I sang along at about a fourteen-acre volume. By noon I had moved forty-seven thousand pounds of hay and had only a dusty face and panache with a two-tined hayfork to show for it.

11

A MAN JOINS REGGIE and me at the barbed wire along
278 in the Big Hole. We are from New York. He is
from Indiana, where he owns two pet shops, but he
grew up in the Madison Valley near Ennis, Montana,
and made hay with overshot stackers as a boy. There is
just no point asking how a man gets from haying at
McAtee Bridge to owning two pet shops in Indiana.
The same illogic of will and desire accounts for the
woman in this man's van who waves with one hand and
holds a Shih Tzu in the other. A Shih Tzu, if asked how
he got from Indiana to the Big Hole, could at least say
he was carried.

The Indiana man identifies the grasses. "Here's nutgrass and bluestem, and see that tall cylindrical stuff over there, that's timothy. There's some redtop. That dark green clump is sloughgrass." He tells us a story about an antelope that ran down one of the deep irrigation ditches dried for haying. Only its pronghorns rose above the earth. The man from Indiana falls silent, elbows on the barbed wire, and watches the work in the hayfield to the east. Then he heads to the van, whose tires soon hiss down the road.

A fire has been burning for days in the Salmon Valley across the Bitterroots. The prevailing winds have whisked its smoke into the Big Hole, and the gray hangs low enough to obscure those familiar peaks in the west, making the terrain seem flat-out wide. Somehow the smoke and the dry July air have changed the properties of light. The haycrews work against a two-dimensional gray-green scrim. When fire isn't searing Idaho, the Big Hole landscape deepens endlessly; after the eye has taken in the blunt, unitary evidence of the mountains, draws and gulches and talus slopes continue to emerge into sight. Today, everything between the distance and the barbed wire has been foreshortened by smoke.

Sound has grown deceptive too. Eyes attest to activity in the field from which ears expect to hear a steady roar arising. But there is only the infrequent bullsnort of a Caterpillar whose exhaust stack adds to the haze. A buckrake peels off from the swirl of activity a quarter mile away and roars around a corner close to us. Its engine cuts in and out as it changes angle to our ears; even once the sound of skidding hay is audible. On the buckrake sits a vision of ranch romance. She wears a well-beaten straw hat, mirrored sunglasses, white T-shirt, and from the front looks taut and tan. When she corners I see a golden braid running down her back like a second spine. Smoky dreams of making hay.

The buckrake loses momentum, so with a quick brown hand she slips the shiftstick into reverse, slides back a few yards, then rams ahead into the haypile. A nimbus of dust washes over the buckrake. She tears across the field, backing off and butting the haypile again and again as it grows. On an inside track behind her comes a wheelrake towed by an ancient Farmall C with a youngster in a batting helmet at the wheel. He slows at the corner, raises the rake's tined wheels, turns and drops them again, then heads down the edge of mown hay. The silent wheelrake looks, to my imagination, as if it should make a *snick snick snick snick snick* sound. In a while Ranch Romance makes another circuit, this time tighter to the center.

Time changes at the barbed wire. On the highway, the cars rushing past with trans-state velocity share the clock conventions of the Indiana man: spring forward, fall back, standard time in winter months only. Nine A.M. first Monday in May, his pet shops open when the sun is fifteen degrees lower in the sky than at nine A.M. on the last Saturday in April. The dogs are still drowsy when he gets to work. But in the Big Hole, out there on the benches, time rests entirely on when the dew rises. No point having a crew of heavy eaters awake and active at seven in the morning if the dew evaporates at eleven Daylight Savings Time. So in summer ranchers of the Big Hole dispense with convention. They remain on Mountain Standard, and some set their clocks back an extra hour to Big Hole time. At ten in the rest of the

Rocky Mountains, it can be eight in the Big Hole and the grass will be dry. The hay finally stacked in early August, the clocks leap ahead and the days yawn forward.

When the grass headed in late July, a week or so after the water disappeared, teams of mowers drove onto the hayfields. Some pulled single sickle-bar mowers, others the new double-wides from Jackson. As the crop fell neatly behind, the mowers earned the mysterious satisfaction that comes from cutting grass, something even shirtless suburban boys feel tackling a neglected lawn. It is like polarizing the graminous creation: the cut reduces stray reflections off supple blades to consistency, and the crewcut stiffness of newmown grass refracts a darker green. When mowing is over in the Big Hole and man has acted the part of fire, the shining stems lie flat and even on the ground and the sun glances off the fields with a silver light. Up close, in hand, the grass (even bluejoint and redtop) is still as green as ever, and it stays that way deep in the stack.

Just beyond the wire and the main ditch and the dark sloughgrass and the wobbling heads of timothy, the boy in the batting helmet has hopped off his tractor to replace a couple of tines on the wheelrake he is towing. Conventional midwestern siderakes are ground-driven by a set of gears linked to one of their two tires. Big Hole wheelrakes have no gearing at all. On the giant raking wheels, tines bend slightly at the middle. As the tips of its tines catch the earth, each wheel revolves and pitches hay onto the next wheel and the next wheel and the next wheel until the hay drops off the side of the rake in a windrow. Every now and then, a tine pitches into the earth too steeply and snaps. The boy loosens a couple of nuts, pulls a spare pair of tines out of the toolbox on the tractor, and bolts them in place. He is away, the buckrake on the windrow outside him a little closer to his tail.

STANDING AT THE wire, waiting for Ranch Romance to orbit again, I watch a planetary system on edge. When one green haytool leaves my ken, some other moving body flames into sight surrounded by an aureole of dust and Salmon Valley smoke. The first path belongs to a pair of wheelrakes at opposite sides of the field. They spiral inward leaving windrows in their wakes. Buck-rakes whirl behind them, shoving windrows to a depot in front of the beaverslide. There an older hand on a buckrake heaves back and forth, loading hay onto the basket. Perpendicular to the beaverslide sits the hoist, a converted buckrake, winding and unwinding steel cables on a pair of tire-size metal bobbins. The cables whip and sing like a fly line with a thirty-pound steelhead at the hook. The basket rises and falls.

Like Venus, Ranch Romance fills a hot niche in the field. The hoist man anchored to his spot, the wheel-rakers tied to the symmetry of the fencelines, and the crazyrakers, just babies, all obey a hierarchy of responsibility and age. Buckrakers flash about like retrograde planets, following the windrows but repeatedly backing and slamming, careening off in pursuit of a buffalo hump of hay. They run as fast as the terrain and the grass-mound ahead of their tined scoop lets them. They have more fun than any other group in agriculture except

Nelson the Simmenthal and Red Nuts the Limousin when they join the heifers at pasture in July. Buckrakers have a hard time looking sober, one of the reasons Ranch Romance wears mirrored sunglasses.

A buckrake is halfway to what Don Garlits would do with a one-ton Chevy truck if he kept its good, lugging engine. It is a modest, stiff-framed dragster with front-wheel drive built not for tar quarter-miles but for slick, uneven ground. The engine sits behind the driver, because the driver faces backward on a steel tractor-seat. The differential has been inverted and reversed so the truck backs up through all forward gears. The body, the box, the interior and all extraneous parts have been scrapped. A buckrake's only allusion to haying is the hydraulics that lift and lower the wooden rake bolted to a welded frame ahead of the double front tires. When the rebuilding is done, they prime it, paint it, put a golden woman at the wheel, and point it toward cattle fodder turning silver in the sun.

I am caught at the wire of some barrier I can't explain. A few steps behind Reggie and me runs 278, flat and black as a cast-iron skillet, down the eastern bench of the Big Hole to Jackson. A road like that is never local. Nothing is as universal as asphalt. At Rose's Cantina in Jackson, hot water from the springs (by which Clark and Sacajawea once camped) fills the toilet bowls. For lunch, we ate ranchburgers and chicken rice soup beside highway women—blaze-vested signholders—recruited from town for some roadwork near the entrance to the Forty Bar. They are locals in a local place (Andy the gingerly cook is their friend) but they have brought with them to Rose's the inexplicable sense that what is

important about highways like 278 is not the here but the there. Every stone in the asphalt leans forward.

Ahead of us, deep into the irrigated bench, the buckrakes and wheelrakes and crazyrakes circle, the buckrakes like square-front snowplows on fodder, the wheelrakes silently snicking along, the crazyrakes provident in corners and odd angles where the slippery grass escapes. They comb the ground, thump over skunk holes, rattle across fords in the shallow irrigation cuts, home in on the beaverslide that sits at the center. Its basket lies on the earth's plane until loaded. Then cocked at right angles to the slide and smoothly raised, wooden teeth carry a twenty-foot rack of hay up and over the top. Another nimbus of dust rises in the cage where the stack, something utterly indigenous, grows in size. Caught at the wire, familiar and unfamiliar with these goings on, I like the probabilities of the field better than the possibilities of the road. But then I am not a local.

As each load of hay falls over the top of the derrick, wisps of longstem grasses float down on a white pickup parked at its base to lend scale to the operation. The ground looks strewn like the road to Jerusalem with palms. Every now and then a boy on the truck's tailgate gets up and tosses a few pitchforks of loose hay onto the basket. Were the hay wetter than it is this noon (two P.M. where I stand), he would add a shovel of salt to each basket load. Salt galls the moisture out of hay and prevents the occasional smoldering of an overripe stack. Seen from our distance, hay falls softly into the cage; from his, it tumbles swiftly with a rushing sound.

Taller than wide, unstable, shaggy-browed, one square column of the stack has been finished. The ground crew opens the side wings of the cage, and it looks as though the edifice will come down on their heads. Part of one wall slips away. The Cat belches a couple of times, pulls in front of the beaverslide, and takes the slack out of the towing cables. It drags the derrick on skids one stack length ahead and reintroduces some slack. The crew folds the wings into place and the next load goes up and over the top to start a new column of grass abutting the old one. A backstop holds up the end of the lengthening stack. In the days before wings and backstops, four men tromped the hay down and rounded the tops. Two men tromped when they used backstops and no wings. Now no men tromp. The boy with the pitchfork climbs onto the stack and fills in depressions where water would collect.

As their young day wears on, the hands in the crew

round off one square column after another. When they have finished four in a line the Cat tows the beaverslide, wings folded forward, into the next hayfield. For nearly two weeks the crews have been haying and evidence of their speed lies all around us. The fields are full of loaflike stacks, some long, some short, all but last year's a succulent green. The Big Hole has become a valley of construction workers laboring in an impermanent medium. If Big Hole ranchers hayed snow in winter, the stacks would stand high into their antipodal season and then slowly melt away. For these summer grasstacks, the antipodal season is winter, when they disappear in dinosaur handfuls at a time, fed by hayforks to the herds.

THEY FINISH ANOTHER field and in no time another until there are no more fields to finish. The grass has all been swept from the earth, its moisture still partly intact, and deposited in great piles that will outreach the snow. It has not been crushed or crimped like Louie's alfalfa, just rearranged, its heliophile vectors abandoned in the chaos of the stack. Mounds of sun and water fill the Big Hole.

First the wheelrakers stop, their paths exhausted. Then the crazyrakers, all the corners clean. Then buckrakers pull into the shade of the last stack and kill their engines. One buckrake still heaves hay onto the basket, and the hoist continues to crank. Then together they stop too, the last load of hay over the top. The boy with the pitchfork climbs onto the stack and shapes the roof, sinking to midcalf in the grass. Everyone watches him for a change. The hoist cables wind up one last time. The Cat driver waits to have the tow lines hitched. Then he pulls the beaverslide away from the stack and heads slowly down the fields to where the derrick rests in winter. The wheelrakers hydraulically bend their implements so they will fit through narrow gates and the gaps behind sheds. They lead the way onto 278. Pickups, crazyrakes, wheelrakes, buckrakes, and a hoist head north.

In front of us the stack begins to surrender to gravity. It collapses into itself. Internal temperatures will rise slightly. Had a careless crew worked with wet hay, the stack might begin to steam as cold damped the Big Hole; it might, in a truly rare instance, catch fire. But this was a careful crew. If anything the hay was drier than they like. The nubs of bluejoint, fescues, redtop, nutgrass, foxtails, bromegrass, clovers, and timothy recover from the cut and the traffic and reconcile themselves to a short spurt of growth before the freeze. In another month, a pickup will pull onto the fields. A couple of hands will get out and erect wooden fences around the stacks, like pickets around a thatched cottage. Then cattle will flood the fields and bite the grasses down to the nub again.

Rain falls, hail pounds, winds whine, snow drifts. The promontories of hay gain character; they rot some on the surface while their hearts stay green. The grass goes tawny, and the stacks lose their loft. One shoulder slumps while another remains tall. Depressions develop. Sometimes the light bathes them in gold, sometimes it deprives them of color completely. Elk, antelope, and mule deer lip the edges where they can gap or leap the fences. When deep snow raises the valley floor, the stacks look like sediment-embedded boulders dropped by an ancient glacier. When spring comes and the Big Hole melts into a plateau of water, they will only be squatty remnants of themselves.

But ahead of us now, and behind us too, across the

highway, rise rectangular barns built of late-July hay. A motionless hush comes over the landscape. Reggie and I walk to our pickup, parked on the edge of 278, and drive away, a handful of grasses on the seat between us.

We pass the Forty Bar and the roadwork. Two miles north, we catch the implement parade. Wheelrakes and crazyrakes first, their drivers waving at us. Then another half-mile farther north, we reach the buckrakes, who are weaving across the highway for fun. We swing to the left and pass one, then another and another. They roar and sputter, their decks swept clean of grass by the wind. Ranch Romance smiles at the two of us and waves as well. We turn west in Wisdom. We pass the Spokane Ranch and the Rutledge buffalo. By the time we pass the Big Hole Battlefield, where the Nez Perce fought Colonel Gibbon and Alva Noyes tended casualties, the haying crew is home. The Cat is still towing the beaverslide south.

We cross the Bitterroots and hop down into smoky Idaho. We do not stop until the pickup overheats in the driveway of a small ranch. The owner has just returned from working a gold mine in northern California and is doing some repairs around the house. In front of his barn and roadside pasture, the state is laying new asphalt.

12

IN OCTOBER 1945, ELMORE JACK took two snapshots of historic interest. First he photographed Hiroshima's City Hall, one of the few large structures left standing near ground zero where two months earlier an atomic bomb had burst. Then he climbed to its top and photographed the environs. I like to imagine Elmore Jack on that parapet. He was among those, the 41st Infantry, who would have invaded Japan in late summer 1945 had peace not come first. He suffered the kind of war that makes men quiet. And as he stood there trying to contain in his camera's viewfinder the scorched rubble that bled into the outlying hills, he could not have helped thinking about Iowa. In Lyon County, where the corn had grown brittle with ripeness, Hilda waited on the Bruns home place for Elmore Jack's return, a first-born son on her lap and a tractor, bought on time, standing silent in a dark shed. I like to imagine Hilda at her parapet that day too.

I learned these facts forty years later at the VFW lounge in Luverne, Minnesota, a Larry Olsen polka thumping in the background. Elmore Jack leaned over, his bolo tie swung forward, and he gestured with a closed hand as he talked. Ever since I found a wad of yen in a rolltop desk at my grandparents' house and was cautioned against asking too many questions, I have grown up thinking that Elmore Jack does not like to mention his war memories. He has always been a soft-spoken man. His head is leaner than those of most of my paternal relatives, whose faces tend to roundness, and it is dominated by an aquiline nose, the same my brother John inherited. Compared to his nose, Elmore Jack's eyes seem small. He has a sad face, but he smiles while dancing in the huge darkness at the VFW lounge. Perhaps for the same reason, three nights later, he smiles while thumbing his stiff, time-blanched war photos in the kitchen of the Bruns home place where he and Hilda still farm. Before she became a Klinkenborg Hilda was a Bruns.

Hilda offers me a Coke or a Diet Coke or a root beer or lemonade or iced tea or coffee or a Dr. Pepper and a piece of cake or some hard candy she keeps around for her grandchildren. I settle for a Coke. We have before us on the kitchen table a couple of albums and a cigar box full of grinning men in khaki. They have not been out of the attic in decades. The photos lie scattered between Elmore Jack and me like antique playing cards. Elmore Jack narrates in his fuzzy voice and Hilda corrals the information, adding a date here, subtracting a name there. She knits a potholder, the loose ends held firmly in place by her glance, which is sharpened by steel-rimmed glasses.

Hilda keeps busy all the time. Not just at kitchen work, lawnwork, farmwork, and the job of chronicling the whereabouts of her scattered brood. (Two sons farm nearby, another, Keith, lives with his family in Washington D.C., and a daughter, Nadean, works as an oil geologist in Montana.) She keeps her finger-ends occupied. She is a one-woman knick-knack factory. She turns out potholders and Christmas tree ornaments, presenting them modestly. Last Christmas Hilda sent Reggie and me a knitted papilionaceous ornament with a yellow pipe-cleaner hanger. In her card she wrote, "I may put a butterfly in here. It won't hurt you." The first thing Hilda showed me when I came to the house was her 1984 ornament, of which she had assembled dozens. I was sorry not to have received one. They were miniature birdfeeders full of real birdseed. She had made them with used communion cups.

Elmore Jack talks softly about the invasion-readiness of the Japanese, about high-explosives depots and railway tunnels full of airplane engines. A faint, uncharacteristic note of pride charges his voice as he shows me his 41st Infantry yearbook, the campaigns marked in bold, sabre-like arrows. Elmore Jack's unit fought its way north from the Philippines, but most of his service photos resemble those a tourist in Japan might have taken in the late 1930s. A few show exploding Japanese hillsides where arms had been cached. They remind me of snapshots many Iowans took during the late 1950s and early 60s. Old wooden grain elevators had to be pulled down to make way for concrete ones of vastly greater capacity. Some grit-handed, rusty-headed man who had a yard full of heavy machinery would clutch his Cat over the railroad tracks to where the elevator stood, hook a long cable to the top of the building, and with the blessing and authority of the co-op, drive away. To those present—half the town—the elevator must have fallen with an awful crash and a fountain of dust. I only ever saw the photographs, and the effect was disappointing.

We get to talking about the cost of farming. Elmore Jack explains how tough it can be when the price of spring planting reaches a hundred dollars an acre—seed and chemicals and fuel factored in—and you farm more than four hundred acres. Never mind land and equipment costs. In nearly every farmhouse I visited I heard someone say, "I don't know how a young farmer gets started." The older, conservative farmers preserve a shady optimism, what you might feel when your car went off the road and you thanked the Lord you had not been driving in the mountains. As always, the small towns display the most visible effects of the farming slump. "George used to have six car and farm equipment dealerships," Elmore Jack says. "Now there isn't but one." In town that morning I had seen men and women lining up for free cheese. Shops stand empty, luncheonettes close. Hilda sympathizes. "Ya, I always wonder what the bachelor men do."

Elmore Jack is quick to blame no one. "Some of

them farmers," he says, leaning back in his chair, an arm outstretched, "have had plain bad luck, a couple of crop failures in a row or they bought land during the high prices. Most of the fellas who got in trouble did it to themselves though. They take over a farm and they need a new house and a new pickup and new machinery. People wanna live on the farm like they live in town. No wonder they got problems." Hilda nods in agreement over her knitting. Two days earlier, watching Elmore Jack scout some steers, Hilda had remarked, "I said to him, 'EJ, let's not finish cattle this year.' But EJ always wants to give it another try, hoping maybe prices'll come back up. I don't know. He takes care of the cattle so I let him do what he wants."

Despite the bad times, the alfalfa leafs out as green as it ever did in ancient Persia. Unlike Louie, Elmore Jack bales his first cut in small square bales, the kind that prevailed between World War II and the early seventies. (Commercial hay producers, small farmers, and dairy men still favor them, though Elmore Jack doesn't milk. He likes square bales because they're easy to handle.) Tomorrow he will windrow the alfalfa, and by Friday it will be dry. I have asked all my uncles and cousins if I can help them make hay and they have accepted the offer with mixed emotions. Louie, as host, has dibs. But a Vermeer roundbaler saves labor, and in this case mine is the labor saved. Elmore Jack agrees to give me a job for the day.

As we exchange farewells in the cool night air under a cloudless sky, I tell Elmore Jack and Hilda something Hilda's sister Lorraine said to me the week before. Hilda and Lorraine both have the Bruns black eyes and dark complexion and a kind of fierce bluntness. They also have identical voices, deceptively sharp, musical, and high with deep undertones, ready to laugh. I explained to Lorraine that I had come to the Midwest to make hay with my uncles. She sized me up, turned to my dad and said, "What do you think, Ron? Shall we tell him the worst and get it over with?"

"Oh ya," Hilda laughs, "the only thing hotter is shocking oats."

FRIDAY MORNING WHEN Hilda calls and says "EJ's baling today," I'm already wearing my baling clothes—sneakers, a Chouinard T-shirt stained with hydraulic fluid, heavy cotton work gloves, a Pioneer Seed cap, and a pair of jeans with holes in the knees. I pull into Elmore Jack's a half hour later. (When Hilda sees my jeans, she asks, "Who patches your pants? Give'em here, I'll do it.") In the sun-creased yard, Elmore Jack and his first-born, Kerwin, adjust an elevator that rises at a forty-degree angle. (A portable farm elevator is really an escalator. A co-op elevator is a tower for storing grain.) Kerwin and Elmore Jack tug its earth-bound tail back and forth, trying to slide the elevator's nose through an open door high up the front of the barn. A pair of hands reaches out and pulls it into place. Kerwin yells, "How's that look?" "OK fine," shouts the voice belonging to the hands. Dale, Elmore Jack's youngest son (just a year my junior), climbs through the door, tosses his legs over the elevator's aluminum-gray rail, and slides sidesaddle to earth. I say hi. My uncle and two cousins greet me with a look that barely conceals their instinctive feeling

that trouble comes in not a less beguiling form than that of a townboy with innocent intentions. I know the look well. Everon used it once when I crashed the Farmall B into the threshing machine.

Kerwin, hatless, wears short brushed hair and a madras plaid short-sleeved shirt. His nearly oriental eyes float on high cheekbones. Kerwin belongs to a genuine Iowan ecotype, vintage 1960, a time when to be tall, well-mannered, and quiet carried an inordinate amount of authority even with short, rude, and noisy boys. Every Future Farmers of America chapter in the state claimed a couple of young men like Kerwin, serious, as they were tall, before their time. They grew up, married, entered the service, begat children, bought a farm not far from where they were raised, and now, in partnership with their fathers and (sometimes) younger brothers, farm the home place too. Their younger brothers have usually pursued more oblique careers because a form of primogeniture prevails in farming families and because the agricultural debt crisis has nullified many traditional assumptions. At first Kerwin seems impatient. Next to Dale, he does not look conspicuously strong. Next to me he does.

Elmore Jack hooks the elevator to the power take-off of a pale-green John Deere old enough to have an exposed steering linkage. (A power take-off, or PTO, is essentially a geared-down extension of a tractor's crankshaft; linked to a universal-joint coupling, it powers all sorts of towed or mounted implements from the rear of the tractor.) That done, the elevator is ready to haul hay to the loft. An administrative pow wow occurs. The windrowed alfalfa will be dry in another three hours, after dinner, about one. Kerwin and Dale can finish cultivating the forty-acre cornfield next to the hayfield. Elmore Jack has plenty to do around the farmyard. And me? The mudslide of technology has made a townboy even more useless than he is by nature. On a hayrack I can ruin only my hands, but until they get me on a hayrack I remain a problem. Everyone relaxes when I volunteer to drive one of the simpler tractors, anything smaller than a Spanish galleon. They decide to hitch me to a siderake.

In the machine shed only thin vertical slats of space stand vacant. Two huge International Harvester tractors and their cultivators consume half the shed. An IH combine crowds the roofbeams. "Did you ever see one of these?" Kerwin asks. He points to a mirror mounted low on the frame of his tractor. It is a device called Culti-Vision, which sounds like a cable network for Rajneeshees, but is exactly what it appears to be, a simple mirror. It allows Kerwin to keep the cultivator (which trails behind) aligned in the corn rows by looking down and forward rather than down and back. After a moment's calculation we shift nose weights from tractor to tractor. The weights themselves are preposterously small compared to the bulk of the machines; adding one to the snout of an eight-ton tractor to improve its draw seems as absurd as putting pennies in one's loafers to gain traction.

Kerwin and Dale start their engines and abruptly depart, cultivator wings folded, some sense of a brotherly race in the making.

Elmore Jack and I climb onto his IH 656 (just like Louie's except for its wide-spread front tires) and drive to the grove, a lane flanked by machinery and trees. We detach the sprayer (like everyone else this week, Elmore Jack has been using 2,4-D and Banvel) and hitch up the New Holland siderake, a plain implement that requires no hydraulics or PTO couplings, only a couple of levers to adjust its height.

While Elmore Jack drives, I sit on the tractor's left fender, a practice all farm-equipment manufacturers warn against. Grandchildren regularly plummet from this post to their deaths under gruesome devices. Sitting there I feel precariously young, especially since Elmore Jack is about to conduct a brief tutorial on siderake operation. We pass feed grinders, feed wagons, mowers, augers, grain drills, corn planters, plows, disks, harrows, manure spreaders, and drive onto a small field of bromegrass and orchardgrass just west of the windbreak shielding the house.

The day ascends into beauty. For some reason the first line of a George Herbert poem comes to mind: "Rise Heart, thy Lord is risen." The eastern sun has not warmed this field. Cool, dense air, dark in shadow, clings to it. A slender fringe of unmowed grass skirts the fenceline and catches the wind in its heads. Beyond the shaded field, the landscape lies open to light like a body of water. A pickup skims along the gravel road that borders the field on the north, for a moment raising a rattle of stones and a tail of lucent dust. Two miles to the northwest lies Everon's place, and Janelle and Louie's to the northwest farther still. Due west two miles sits Edna, a hamlet. Beneath my seat, a great tire turns like a waterwheel, churning dew into light. From under the oaks of the grove I see penumbral country all around.

"Hold on," Elmore Jack shouts over the exhaust

133

roar. "We used to keep hogs in this field and they rooted it up pretty good." (Descendants of those free-running porkers now live in confinement at Kerwin's, like princes in the Tower. It can truly be said that there was once a better time to be a hog.) I turn to watch the siderake. As it moves forward on rubber tires, two offset circular disks mounted at either end of the siderake rotate at a sharp angle away from the direction of travel. Tined bars stretch between these disks, and when the siderake advances the tines describe a circle parallel to them, combing the earth. If you want to rake hay away from the field's edge (in) you travel clockwise; if you want to rake hay toward the edge (out) you move in a counterclockwise direction.

The dew still lies thick on this shaded field. We bounce from one end to the other, turning over a slug trail of damp grass. Elmore Jack handles the tractor by pure touch. He keeps his head turned to watch the windrow behind us. The 656 reads the terrain ahead. We make one round of the field and then speed down a dirt track to the alfalfa.

"No point windrowing the orchard grass," says Elmore Jack. "Sun won't hit that field till noon. Think you know how to run this thing?"

"Uh huh," I assure him. I am looking at fourteen acres of alfalfa, narrow and deep, enclosed by other fields.

"Fine. This field's already been windrowed out. Why don't you windrow it in?"

Elmore Jack hops off and walks away without waiting to see if I will make a mistake. I do some quick figuring to decide which direction I should travel and whether I am supposed to siderake around the field or up and down. The answers, obviously, are clockwise and around. A farmboy would not have to wonder. The tractor would make the decision for him. That is one problem with being a townboy: you are cut off from the mental life of machines.

I decide clockwise means south, west, north, and east, in that order. Unlike Louie's alfalfa field, Elmore Jack's has little grade. It dips slightly. From the southern end, the gravel road to the north forms the horizon. From the northern end, you have the faint sense of a view developing to the south. With undue caution (sideraking is one of the simplest tasks in farming) I begin my rounds. This is not, after all, a trackless wilderness. I just have to follow the leguminous path.

Behind me hay tumbles. I steer the guide tire (front left) just beyond the left side of the windrow and everything falls into place. At first, I move slowly and the alfalfa barely flops on its side. But as the 656 takes more throttle the siderake starts to swish loudly. An endlessly breaking wave crests and falls behind me. When you drive down a country road and see windrowed hay lying out in the fields, it seems to cling to the stubble, to be a level disturbance of color. But when you rake it, the tines lift it up, pass it along to the right, and stand it on edge in a high line. The meaning of windrow—a row through which wind blows—becomes clear.

It is something of a miracle that I am sideraking at all. Most farmers who own windrowers no longer siderake. Though it shortens drying time, it also causes additional leaf loss. And by eliminating sideraking, farmers reduce the hours spent in the field. There is no doubt that fieldwork, even on a modern tractor, grows repetitive. No question that drudgery sets in. But to his infrequent farm visits, a townboy brings the gift of shallowness and a nose for novelty. I cannot feel the deep round of sameness in windrowing. As it happens, I rarely tractor across the earth's mantle, pressed down by a June sky, rousing a sibilant stiff surf behind me. Routine entombs minor pleasures, and I have left routine far away. There is no glory in this fun, only dumb delight.

West of me, Kerwin and Dale fly up and down the rows of corn, cultivators streaking the air with dust. Once, Dale traverses a narrow fencegap to work on the next field over. As he threads his way between fenceposts, his many-speared implement rises from the soil and collapses hydraulically to half its working width, then unfolds again and settles down to cleaning corn. Barn swallows, air-trout, arc around my tractor, ferreting insects out of their panicked trajectories. Blackbirds and a crow quarrel at the southeast corner. Five rows in, I can see that the sideraked swaths have already lightened to a pale green. The inner ones stay dark with moisture.

An hour passes. Several pickups run by. A checkered Edna Cooperative Feed truck crosses the north.

On a turn at the field's far end, the steering suddenly goes dead. I have flattened a front tire. This, to me, has the appearance of inevitability. I had a level field, simple machinery, and an easy task. I planned to cause no snickering. It might have been worse. The steering linkage could have snapped and the throttle jammed, causing me to siderake every crop between here and the next deep ditch. A clutch of farmers would circle the wreck saying, "Never saw anything like it. You ever?"

I stalk around the tractor in disgust and suddenly hear silence coming from the field west of me. This *is* worse. Kerwin has stopped his tractor and run to the fence. "You OK? What happened?" he shouts as loudly as he can. "Flat tire," I scream. "Need a ride back to the house?" he shouts. "Nope," I yell back. It is hard to yell "nope" indifferently, but, Jesus, at least I know how to walk. Unless I put a nail through my foot. Or my hair catches fire.

But somehow this is where I have wanted to be all along, square in the middle of a farm section with the tractor shut down. Around me, tilled land boxes the compass. The stubble-field wheels through the atmosphere and a southerly breeze arises. I face into the wind and a booming echo assails my ears. I feel like I am being squashed against the sky, a diminutive bug on a divot in a *bleu céleste* saucer. The sun falls forcefully into the wind-hollows, raising sweat on my arms and brow. We are reaching the time of day when the earth sheds its chroma. I step over row after row of dry-leaved alfalfa. By the time I reach the dirt road, Lorraine's words ("Shall we tell him the worst?") make perfect sense. It is a prime haying day. Hot.

Elmore Jack cannot be found. I check the barns and the machine shed and the house. Hilda thinks he came to look for me. His pickup pulls into the garage. Elmore Jack closes the driver's door. "Run out of gas? I forgot to check the gauge." I explain the situation, including the possibility that I may have destroyed the tire by daydreaming. "Hell," he says, "it was an *old* tire." (They were old daydreams too.) By the time we have changed the tire, it is dinnertime. Noon.

YOU KNOW YOU HAVE hit country when you can't get to the kitchen from the back door without passing a small sink. How much humus reaches the Mississippi Delta through small Cornbelt sinks has never been calculated in soil erosion studies. When you work with clean white stuff like paper all day, you get out of the habit, dear to mothers, of washing your hands before each meal. After a few days on a farm you cannot think of food without thinking first of a shallow porcelain bowl and some hard, strong soap.

Elmore Jȧck, Kerwin, Dale, and I wash up and (the word springs to mind) traipse in for dinner laid in the air-conditioning up a set of steps to the kitchen. The cool feels good. An L (counters, sink, and stove) encloses the table on two sides, and a small office nook lies open on another. Food fills the table and counters. Baked potatoes, sour cream, butter, white bread, margarine, jam, milk, lemonade, asparagus, string beans, ketchup, and a chuck roast. Beside the chuck roast lie three sorry wieners. "This cut had too much bone," Hilda says, "so I cooked up some hot dogs too. You just help yourselves."

We eat with silent dedication. Hilda works on her potholders, a selfless act since the first ones she was ever given, now singed and mutilated, hang above the stove. To the refrigerator's side stick photos of all kinds, grandchildren and recent Dutch guests. Next to them hangs a tiny crank telephone made by a man whose hands were distorted in an accident. We start to talk about haying. Kerwin wonders why Louie roundbales his first cut. ("We get too much rain early in the summer; round bales don't keep well through all that wet.") But then Louie might wonder why Elmore Jack and Kerwin side-rake. I tell some New York stories. We talk about Washington, Germany, and Montana. The noon news floats in from the living-room TV. Hilda gets up, turns the living-room set off, and clicks on the one over Elmore Jack's desk. We listen to hog and corn futures as we eat.

The thread of an old discussion emerges. Should a farmer bank on his crops or play the futures game too, both ends of the market? The question evokes some equivocation. The answer depends entirely on the state of the market, Congress, the strength of prices, the weather. No assurances can be had, as Janelle and Louie found when their financial adviser persuaded them to buy soybean futures. Dale, getting up from the table with an air of finality, says, "Farming may be an unsure way to go broke, but futures is a sure way." He lies back in a recliner in the living room.

Hilda offers more food and drink, but dinner is over. We arrange to swap tractors. Kerwin will take the 656 and hitch it to the baler, and I will finish sideraking on a new, hydrostatic John Deere. Elmore Jack will grease the baler. We descend the steps to the sink, pick up our gloves (and my hat) and walk full-face into the spine-prickling day. Elmore Jack shows me around the John Deere, parked, fortunately, in the scant shade of the barn. Hydrostatic tractors are built for townboys and retired insurance salesmen with a couple of acres in garden. They require no shifting. The John Deere has two levers, one to choose forward or reverse, another, the throttle, marked with a rabbit (fast) and a turtle (slow). Were it not that the baler needs the 656's horsepower (but not as much as the giant tractors generate), I would feel demoted. Elmore Jack and Kerwin look at the old John Deere coupled to the elevator. "We should give you that one," says Elmore Jack with a smile. "It's got a hand clutch."

ANOTHER HOUR TO FINISH sideraking. The day will reach a hundred degrees easily. The breeze has begun to choke, and heat shimmers off the John Deere's hood. It doesn't bother the barn swallows. I am at the far end of the alfalfa when the baling crew heaves into view, chugging down the dirt access road. Elmore Jack drives the 656. Behind the tractor, in a long straggling line, come the baler and three hayracks hitched together, Kerwin and Dale leaning idly against the back of the first one. They fill the field where I have been working.

Every person I know in the Midwest agrees that haying is hot, heavy, and dirty work. I have had a hard time explaining my interest in it to them and to myself. Until this moment of Elmore Jack's, Kerwin's, and Dale's arrival, the closest I had come to a satisfactory account was this: I never, when I was a boy, understood what my uncles actually did during the summer and I wanted to know. There are other reasons. I like the smells and the weather and the idea of haying. Square-baled alfalfa harvests a satisfying bulk, stored, unlike other crops, in a big barn, not mingled anonymously at the local coop with every other soybean, corn kernel, or oat in the township. You can climb into the hayloft and visit summer in the dead of winter if you like. And though some industries put alfalfa to exotic uses (as a poultry-feed supplement it provides xanthophyll, which turns chicken skins and egg yolks that delectable yellow), it is really a simple crop. Cows eat it, and we eat the cows. Haying also summons all the epiphanies I have ever had. They occurred while I stood on the edge of a field across a railroad spur line, my back to a small town, staring at farmsteads off in the distance.

But a finer reason for wanting to hay with my uncles occurs to me now. It lies in the difference between a steel behemoth scratching the soil, its operator shrouded in insulation, and three men moving slowly onto a field with wagons made of wood. Unlike most modern field tasks, haying in Elmore Jack's old-fashioned way is mainly a human, and not a mechanical, event. A combine ingests corn, soybeans, and oats, and when full it empties its belly into trucks that dump loads through grids in the co-op concrete. Every now and then a farmer or an elevator hand may dab at the grain crop with a feed shovel. Otherwise, no one touches it. In the West, ranchers buy automatic bale wagons to gather bales and eliminate lifting. In the hilly East, dairymen use bale kickers that toss bales high into three-sided hayracks. But not here. Second and third cuts, Elmore Jack roundbales alfalfa and a tractor hauls the cylinders home and lines them up. But not this first cut. This cut takes three hayracks, a baler, a tractor, and as many hands as he can muster.

Elmore Jack chooses the outermost windrow. He drives the IH 656 facing backward. Behind it, powered by the PTO and reaching out to the right, trails a New Holland 273 square-baler, chunking loudly and rhythmically like an artificial heart. Behind the baler rides a hayrack, a white flatbed wagon two and a half bale-lengths wide, slightly longer than four bales laid end to end, with a six-foot backstop. A metal loading chute, supported by chains, extends from the baler over the front of the hayrack. Dale and Kerwin place themselves one to the right and one to the left of the loading chute's lip.

The baler extrudes its first bale in ratchety little motions. A second bale shoves it along. Kerwin and Dale examine critically the early bales; the New Holland can make tighter, heavier, longer, or evener rectangles with a few adjustments. Then they look no more. They swing into the sweet, slow rhythm of baling. At half my speed, tractor and hayrack move like a homecoming float bearing unsteady ingénues. Arms extended, Kerwin plucks a bale from the chute, steps to the rear, and drops it precisely. Dale follows and soon they have built a back wall of twenty bales. Kerwin and Dale point at Elmore Jack, who nods and shouts something to them. They look toward the east and laugh. Kerwin, Dale, and Elmore Jack have farmed this field through decades of crop rotations. How many times has one or the other checked the first bale of summer for tightness and heft? Is there a baling joke they always tell that needs looking to the east for a punchline? Watching them from the top of the field as they cross the bottom and coast the western side, I find it impossible not to desire their sense of place, their deep surrender to time. What a season for capitulation! The sun and the hay, between them, have caught us all up.

142

ELMORE JACK TAKES the John Deere I was using back to the grove where he will park the siderake. A hayrack full of bales stands at the edge of the dirt track. Dale and I pull an empty hayrack over to the baler and hitch it. One foot on the wagon tongue, we climb onto the hayrack. The tractor percusses sharply. Kerwin shifts into gear and aligns the baler pickup on the fourth windrow from the edge, leaving two swaths outside us. The hayrack rocks back and forth, the baler clicks and chugs, a green alfalfa brick slides up the chute toward Dale and me, and Dale grabs it, saying, "You wanna catch it at the top of the chute." There is a balance point just at the lip where the bale, climbing up from the bale chamber, hovers for a split second before it somersaults onto the hayrack. If you seize the bale too soon, you have to lift it over the lip; too late and it is already falling.

I had tossed hay recently. W. Ray and I heaved fourteen bales of second-cut hay out a door on the side of his barn down to Louie, who stacked them in his pickup. The hay had cured well (it was last July's). I could slip my palm under both strings of a bale and pick it up with one hand. A normal bale weighs about fifty-five pounds.

A tactile memory of that day runs down my arm as the first bale with my name on it jerks up the chute. A second bale jerks behind it, and a third is already being pounded into shape. I reach with both hands, grab the bale too soon, lift it over the lip. Before I can gauge the bale's weight, the twine explodes. I become Lucy Ricardo. Dale laughs at the surprise on my face. He reaches down (bales looming), grabs bale fragments—slices of

143

hay—and tosses them into the next windrow. In a moment I understand: the baler will rebind the fragments when we reach that windrow. I throw some alfalfa too. Dale grabs a bale. His explodes.

Next turn, I am ready. At the precise moment of balance, I grab the bale. This time weight registers. We are haying on Saturn. I can barely sling the bale to the back of the rack.

"Are these bales heavy?" I ask Dale.

"Ninety-five, a hundred pounds. This windrow's too wet."

Dale tries to wave Kerwin to an outer row, drier by an hour or so. Kerwin shouts back, "In a minute." A minute will be too long. I haul another bale to the back of the rack. It is like dragging a dead man from river mud by his suspenders. Even Dale grunts, to my satisfaction.

We finish the second layer of the back wall. I confess to Dale that I will not be able to lift hundred-pound bales four feet in the air more than twice. He squares the third row. Then, as if to drive home the point that we are baling wet hay, a supporting beam beneath the rear of the hayrack cracks. Dale shouts at Kerwin again, and this time the 656 halts. The hayrack's hindquarters droop. Dale and I rebuild the bale stack to remove some weight from the broken timber.

WE SET OUT AGAIN with a sound, empty hayrack. This time Kerwin takes the outermost swath. These bales come crisp, stems broken not bent, rustling to the touch. They hoist nicely. I am good for the bottom, second, third, and fourth layers, a whole rack, eighty bales, full. Dale shows me how to "tie in" a hayrack. Conventional midwestern square bales are twice as long as they are wide. We stack them in layers of five: two pair side by side the long way across the width of the rack, a single bale (running lengthwise along the edge of the hayrack) laid against their ends. The next layer, we change directions, the lengthwise bale set on the opposite side. Stacked this way, the longitudinal side bales will not tumble off the rack. We make four piles of twenty each.

Dale is a thickset, big man, his strength emphasized by a striped, sleeveless shirt. Like many of the farmers in my family, his musculature is well-sheathed. His arms look misleadingly casual, tucked and rolled like the Naugahyde of a vintage T-bird. Over the years, he has shed like an armored husk the Blakean strength his vain teenage neighbors wear for a Venetian girth of muscle and fat. He handles bales as if they were hollow. We agree that today would be a good day to be out on one of the lakes (Spirit, Okoboji) with some cold beer in the livewell. The thought arrives through the day's heat and the rocking of the hayrack.

I learn not to lift with my biceps. Instead I use my gloved hands as bale-hooks and hold my arms straight, leaning back from the waist to lever the hay before me. Like Dale, I borrow the bale's momentum, swinging it in a pendulum arc from the chute's lip to the stack. It is easier to throw a bale than to lift it.

In the heat, a laziness comes over us despite the pounding of the baler. I feel my way into Dale's rhythm, and Dale decides that I am not going to die of sunstroke or pitch backward off the edge of the rack. Crossing the bottom of the field, Kerwin has relaxed too. The tractor steers itself. The only thing working frenetically is the baler. Its pickup snatches the windrow, rolling it back into the grasp of fingers that rake the hay (perpendicularly to the swath) into the path of a rectangular, knived piston. The piston plunges back and forth, eighty strokes a minute, slicing the continuous web of hay into small pallets and pounding them into the bale chamber. (The knifing action splits individual bales into neat, separate slices. If hay were not sliced, the baler would produce a densely matted block of hay, difficult to feed out to individual cows, who rarely eat an entire bale at one sitting.) The bale nearly ready, two needles impale the hay, baling-twine in their eyes. Intricate knotters grab the twine and tie double overhand knots. A narrow metering wheel stabs the bale in the back and revolves as the bale twitches up the chute and into our tired hands. Slip clutches, flywheels, sprockets and yards of chain, worm gears, bill hooks and springs engage in a seamless rush of mechanical power. The chains rattle, the gears hum, and the plunger thumps. The hayrack creaks. The sky begins to haze up with heat, like an egg's albumen cooking.

WE HAVE ALL HAD two glasses of lemonade and a piece of cake. The kitchen is almost too cold. In the past hour the density of my arms has changed. I am soaked in chilling sweat, sunburned, with dirt in my ears and alfalfa chaff in my nose. Hilda tells how once, while shocking oats, Elmore Jack fainted. I have had a slack spell or two myself today. Kerwin's wife, Nette, drops off their four children and a neighbor boy, Arnie Timmer, two of whom will join the baling crew. Chad, the oldest boy, has cracked an ankle bone and will spend the afternoon watching stories with Hilda. Heidi, wearing a Honey Bear T-shirt, will drive the 656, Chris will help his father stack bales on the hayrack. Matthew and Arnie will fool around. Elmore Jack teases Arnie ("Who's that little girl?") about his tightly curled hair. Arnie's parents had given him a choice: cut your hair or get it permed. Arnie, the eight-year-old farmboy, chose a perm.

CATTLE PENS, POLE barns, machine sheds, the house, the barn, and the grove intercept the breeze and prevent it from cooling the yard. Nothing intercepts the sun. Packed dirt heats like asphalt. Kerwin and Dale wait in the hayloft. Elmore Jack and I stand atop the first of two hayracks that need unloading before Kerwin and the kids can start baling again. Like a giant check-mark, the elevator descends from the barn to the ground, where the old John Deere powers it, and rises to the top of the hayrack, where we load it with bales. An endless pair of spiked bicycle chains with steel rungs between them hooks the bales and slides them up the trough.

I work too fast. We unload the broken rack full of wet hay first, and I want to rush through it so we can get to the bales of normal weight. Elmore Jack slows me down. "You gotta wait," he says, "till the bale hits the bottom of the slide and starts climbing to the barn before you toss another bale on the elevator. Otherwise you make 'em work too hard up there." Last winter, Elmore Jack, who is in his mid-sixties, had a bad bout

147

of pneumonia, from which he is still recovering, and lost more than twenty pounds. The overweight bales do not seem to bother him at all. He wears heavy forest-green twill pants and a twill long-sleeved shirt he keeps buttoned at his wrists. He does not seem hot. (I am grateful about now for the holes in the knees of my jeans.) I ask Elmore Jack about his shirt. "Keeps my arms from getting scratched," he says. I look down at my own arms. Where they are not brown-red with sun, they are blood-red with a thousand tiny etchings.

We unload two wagons, a hundred and sixty bales. Given the conditions, at least ten thousand pounds of alfalfa. Kerwin climbs down out of the hayloft, picks up Chris, Heidi, and the empty hayracks and heads off to the hayfield. Dale, Elmore Jack, and I take another short break. Then I replace Kerwin in the hayloft.

IN THE DAYS NOT so long ago when all farmers milked and the white glazed-brick creameries in small towns had not closed and milk tanktrucks still toured the rural routes, there were, as everyone knows, two lively times in the day of a barn—morning and evening, when cows wandered up from pasture for some artificial nursing: swishing of milkers, slap of hooves, flopping of manure, clank of head-gates, the rasping of an old bakelite radio (that goes on with the lights) set high on the wall between the joists.

Milking took about four out of twenty-four hours. The rest of the day the barn stood empty, idle. If you came to the barn from the chicken-coop, choking with dust and hen clatter, or the hoghouse, with its ceaseless abrupt piglet tides, the barn exhaled vacancy. A cat sleeping on a sill, a barn-swallow fluttering in the eaves, a calf licking itself beside its Holstein mother only added to the sense of idleness. Strangely, if you walked from the barn to the farmhouse in mid-afternoon, say about two-thirty, you would notice there the same idle atmosphere. The house was vacant too. A terrible loneliness would come over you, for you felt that all the human beings on this place had gathered in a tight circle in the corner of a distant field to work on some absorbing problem soluble only by the wisdom of farmers. At least that is what you would feel if you were a townboy.

But a barn is also a cathedral where visiting townboys come to worship farm life. It has the well-rubbed wood of a reverenced church rail, the grain raised by the protruberant hides of quietly agnostic cows. In the hayloft you learn the meaning of motes and beams. You walk across its plank floor, head tilted back. Day outside finds cracks in the roof and walls of the hayloft, and light streaks through the darkness on missions of grace and accusation. The barn is wired to God's wrath by a lightning rod.

When the loft is full of hay you can climb to the roof and examine the rafters, or you can sit with feet dangling out an upper door and watch the ridgepole backs of the dairy herd gathered by the stone foundation far below you. When you climb the ladder to the hayloft, you always pause just as your head and shoulders clear the floor. Your lower body, cut off from sight, seems to grow eyes of its own; your knees can see the look of the lower barn, your loins intuit the spiderwebs that carpet the ceiling. Above, the height of the hayloft seems to suck you into dimness as old as the last cut of hay.

By May the hayloft is usually empty except for a few corrupt straw-colored bales. The alfalfa scaffolding on which, during late August, you clambered to the ceiling's peak and swung from the cables has been eaten, digested, shat, and spread on the fields. When time comes to store new bales, the hayloft doors, front and back, are thrown open, and the great peak door is let down. The upper barn becomes a cavity of light. The elevator pokes into one of the doors, and if you are quick enough you can ride it from the ground to the loft, slide back down, and ride it up again.

During winter and spring, the loft was emptied from the back, bales dumped down the ladder trapdoor. It will be filled in from the front. Bales ride into the barn and are squared in a loosely rectangular stack against the front wall, layer after layer paving the floor upward. As the stack grows, a ladder-like elevator extension is needed to carry the hay farther to the rear, past wasps' nests and piles of coon scat. No number of open doors can ventilate the hayloft. As bales begin to mount up, one wagonload after another, the air gets closer, and chaff displaces oxygen. Hay starts to crowd out the light.

Windrowed, dessicated, raked and baled, Alfalfa, Queen of Legumes, comes home on a hayrack, climbs to the barn on a chain-driven slide, bumps off the elevator and onto the extension, and dives into space. A bale hits the hayloft floor, bounces twice, and skids to a stop at my feet. I pick it up and drag it into the bale-length gap between trusses. Dale catches the next bale on the bounce and flings it next to mine. I try to imitate his ease, but I have begun to stagger a bit in the heat and closeness. Dale shows compassion. Every fifth or sixth bale he takes my turn, telling me while he does so about hunting in Montana, skiing in California, the year he sold his pickup and bought a ticket for the Orient. He is restless. "If I was a landowner," he says, waiting for a bale to drop, "I wouldn't raise livestock. Just crops. Be gone from November till April every year."

We look out the back door to fields beyond the cattleyard. From inside the barn, the sky looks like a river of coolness. The short corn is just assuming the dark green of summer. "Ya, them coons," Hilda said during one of our lemonade breaks, "always getting in the sweet corn. We planted some in the seed corn just to hide it one year and the coons got it all anyway."

After the third or fourth wagonload, we have raised the floor of hay four bales high. Walking on this tessellated surface is treacherous. I have become a danger to myself. When I sling bales I forget to let go and their momentum pulls me over onto the soft, prickly pavement. As I wobble, bale in hands, across deep green hummocks, I forget to watch my step. My leg dives down a hole where the corners of bales do not join. I roll my load vaguely into position. "This isn't precision stacking," says Dale. It's a good thing. I am no longer capable of precision. The roof gradually closes in on us. We stoop. From time to time, one of us crawls over the high stack of bales in the front (just barely higher now than the stack of bales in the back) to see how Elmore Jack is doing in the yard. The wagon always looks three-fourths full.

But as we turn to watch another bale bump onto

the extension, the elevator stops. The old John Deere shuts down. I scramble to the front of the extension and unplug it. Dale and I peer down from the peak of the barn. Elmore Jack leans against an empty hayrack. "Whyn't you come on down?" he shouts. We climb out onto the elevator, its rails hot through our gloves. I throw my Pioneer Seed cap to the ground. We hang for a moment at the top of the elevator, snuffing up the breeze that swirls around the roof.

As I LEAVE, HILDA hands me a large envelope. Inside is a pair of knitted potholders. "Hope you and Reggie can use these, honey," she says. "If you can't, just give'em to somebody else." Elmore Jack, Hilda, and Dale walk me to the car (Kerwin is still in the alfalfa). The two men say, almost at the same time, "Thanks for the help." I say "Thanks for the work." Everybody waves and I pull out of the drive and head west. Just past the grove and the field of bromegrass and orchard grass, I slow and look south. The alfalfa is hidden behind corn. I raise a plume of dust for Kerwin to see.

Two sections west I turn north. I pass Everon's farm—the schoolhouse pasture, the cowlane, the home place, big white house back in the trees. Davis is stacking bales on a hayrack in the field just west of the house. In a cornsheller headed south, Myron and Everon pass me, slowing for the turn into the farm. I come to Highway 9 and turn west to Rock Rapids. Just past the hat factory on its outskirts, I turn north to Janelle and Louie's.

Detached ranch houses line the road from Rock Rapids. I bump down onto the asphalt that runs straight to the Minnesota border a few miles ahead. I pass a cloven farm, barn and sheds on one side of the road, house and garage on the other, Oliver tractors (a fairly uncommon make) parked all around.

In the back of my mind I can hear the voices of Janelle and Louie on their evening drives after dinner. "Shouldn'ta tilled that hillside," Louie would say. "Look at how dirty that field is, Louie," Janelle would say. Or "I wonder how come he's just now windrowing?" Or "There's a nice place; look at that corn." Or "Guy who lives here's always behind; he'll be spraying till midnight." Or "Why don't you buy us some ice cream?" Or "Your dad and I used to play with the kids on that place." Or "Used to be a farmstead over there on that corner; plowed it under a couple years ago." Or "See that place? That acre with a good-condition house, barn, couple of buildings went for nine thousand dollars at auction last year." Or "Old man in that place lived with a woman for forty years; never married her." Or "Louayee!" Or "This guy's been working on that shed for the last three years; looks like he's building a game room for his cows."

Corn, oats, soybeans, and alfalfa whir past. In the last three weeks the crops have fully obscured the soil beneath them, and the landscape has lost every sign of bare-earthed winter. The haze of early afternoon has cleared. Most of the farmers in Lyon County, Iowa, and Rock County, Minnesota, are eating dinner. The car is full of wind. Day begins to tip toward dusk.

Just at the Iowa/Minnesota border, I follow an open curve, a wide bend in the midwestern grid of roads. To the east lies Stateline Church, white clapboard steeple, graveyard, and a gravel parking lot. To the west a long hayfield rises over a hill that forms the horizon. Windrows trace the field's shape like contour-plowed furrows. Half the alfalfa remains unbaled. By the near fence stand a pickup, three tractors, and two filled hayracks. Where the hill leaves the horizon, I can see the Rock River cutting its way through corn and pasture. I stop and watch from a shallow ditch, knee-deep in foxtail barley. A tractor pulling a baler and a hayrack, exhaust wrinkling the light, crests the arc of the field's horizon. In silhouette (for a second) against the sky, two kids with perfect timing pluck bales from the chute. They round the bottom of the field and follow the windrow back up and over the hill. The breeze momentarily catches the baler's chunking sound.

NOTES

p. 43, John Steward's erudite history of the reaper: John Steward, *The Reaper: A History of the Efforts of Those Who Justly May Be Said to Have Made Bread Cheap* (NY: Greenberg, 1931), 171–72.

p. 71, "Alfalfa apparently possesses . . .": J. K. Matsushima, "Role in Feedlot Feeding," in *Alfalfa Science and Technology*, ed. C. H. Hanson (Madison, WI: American Society of Agronomy, 1972), 636.

p. 71, "Because the animal cannot tell . . .": P. J. Van Soest, "Composition, Fiber Quality, and Nutritive Value of Forages," in *Forages: The Science of Grassland Agriculture*, ed. Heath, Barnes, *et al.* (Ames, IA: Iowa State University Press, 1985), 417.

p. 71, twenty-seven million acres: D. K. Barnes and C. C. Sheaffer, "Alfalfa," in *Forages*, 89.

p. 72, "The alfalfa plant . . .": Foster Dwight Coburn, *The Book of Alfalfa* (NY: Judd, 1907), 11.

p. 75, "the papilionaceous corolla": D. K. Barnes *et al.*, "The Flower, Sterility Mechanisms, and Pollination Control," in *Alfalfa Science and Technology*, 123.

p. 77, second largest seed-bearing family: G. H. Heichel, "Symbiosis: Nodule Bacteria and Leguminous Plants," in *Forages*, 64.

p. 77, "the earliest archeological evidence": D. B. Grigg, *The Agricultural Systems of the World* (Cambridge: Cambridge University Press, 1974), 10.

p. 77, "1300 B.C.": J. L. Bolton *et al.*, "World Distribution and Historical Developments," in *Alfalfa Science and Technology*, 5.

p. 79, *aspasti: ibid.*, 4.

p. 79, Lombardy during the twelfth century: Grigg, 137.

p. 79, 1720: B. A. Holderness, "East Anglia and the Fens," in *The Agrarian History of England and Wales*, ed. Joan Thirsk, Volume V, part 1 (Cambridge, Cambridge University Press, 1984), 224.

p. 79, *alfacfacah*: Carl Scofield, "The Botanical History and Classification of Alfalfa," in *Miscellaneous Papers* (1908).

p. 80, "I gave the Lucerne . . .": *Thomas Jefferson's Farm Book*, ed. Edwin Morris Betts (Princeton: American Philosophical Society, 1953), 245.

p. 81, "Lucerne has not succeeded . . .": *ibid.*, 313.

p. 81, As D. K. Barnes . . . writes . . .": D. K. Barnes *et al.*, "Successes and Problems Encountered While Breeding for Enhanced N_2 Fixation in Alfalfa," in *Genetic Engineering of Symbiotic Nitrogen Fixation and Conservation of Fixed Nitrogen*, ed. J. M. Lyons *et al.* (Plenum Publishing Corp., 1981), 234

p. 82, "elicitor and receptor compounds . . . mutual recognition": G. H. Heichel, "Symbiosis," in *Forages*, 65.

p. 82, "after penetration": Barnes, "Successes and Problems," 234.

p. 83, "the major limiting nutrient": *ibid.*, 233.

p. 90, *The Story of Ajax:* Alva Noyes, *The Story of Ajax: Life in the Big Hole Basin* (Helena, MT: State Publishing Co., 1914).